Before Kampuchea

Before Kampuchea

Preludes to Tragedy

MILTON OSBORNE

Orchid Press
Bangkok 2004

Milton Osborne
BEFORE KAMPUCHEA: Preludes to Tragedy

First edition published in 1979 & 1984, by George Allen & Unwin, Sydney
Second edition 2004

ORCHID PRESS
P.O. Box 19,
Yuttitham Post Office,
Bangkok 10907, Thailand

www.orchidbooks.com

Printed in Thailand

ISBN 974-524-044-3

For
Ratsody
and in memory of
Prince Sisowath Entaravong
disappeared April 1975
and
Paulus Tep Im Sotha,
Apostolic Prefect of Battambang
executed April 1975

Friends and guides
to a different Cambodia

Table of Contents

INTRODUCTION TO THE 2004 EDITION

After Kampuchea — Cambodia Twenty-Five Years On

I finished writing *Before Kampuchea* shortly after Pol Pot's tyrannical regime was overthrown at the beginning of 1979, and it was published later that year. When it was reissued in 1984, I saw no reason to change what I had written, but I added a brief 'Postscript'. This took account of two periods I had spent in 1980 and 1981 working as a consultant to the United Nations High Commission for Refugees in relation to the Cambodian refugee problem, and a visit I had made to Cambodia in 1981 at a time when independent foreign visitors were just beginning to be given access to the country.

By 1984 Cambodia was still far from having reached an even a highly qualified semblance of normality. The immediate problem of near famine that had loomed so large in 1979 and 1980 had been overcome, though there were areas of the country where food was still in short supply. The mass refugee exodus that had followed the overthrow of Pol Pot's regime had come to an end. Nevertheless, the fate of more than one hundred thousand refugees in camps in Thailand and elsewhere had still not been solved. Most importantly, Cambodia's political circumstances remained a cause for grave concern as Vietnam's occupation of the country was opposed by ASEAN, China, the United States and its Western allies. As a result Cambodia continued to be a battlefield, with an ongoing guerrilla conflict between the Vietnamese and forces of the Coalition Government of Democratic Kampuchea (CGDK), a government in exile that had been formed in June 1982. In a bitter irony, by far the most effective of the armed forces linked to the CGDK were soldiers of the former Khmer Rouge regime.

1

The man who dominates the story I tell in *Before Kampuchea*, Prince Norodom Sihanouk, was for much of the 1980s an 'on-again off-again' player in Cambodia's political drama. Living for much of the time in Peking or in the isolated calm of the North Korean capital of Pyongyang, he was acutely aware of the ambiguity of his position as the president of a coalition that included the Khmer Rouge. He, after all, had only recently been a prisoner of the Khmer Rouge in Phnom Penh. The formation of the CGDK, he said, was a 'pact with the devil', but a necessary pact to drive out the Vietnamese 'colonisers' of his country. Just as importantly, Sihanouk recognised the demands of *realpolitik* gave him little option but to work with the CGDK, its Khmer Rouge component notwithstanding. His Chinese patrons made clear this was what they required. Moreover, ASEAN, led by Thailand and Singapore, were ready to insist that if he did not cooperate with the CGDK they would not allow him to visit his own partisans located on the Thai-Cambodian border.

By the mid-1980s the situation in Cambodia seemed to be at a stalemate. With few signs that the CGDK forces could oust the occupying Vietnamese, Sihanouk began to talk of the possibility of striking a deal with the Phnom Penh regime headed by Heng Samrin and Hun Sen. In early 1986, and while continuing to insist on the total withdrawal of Vietnamese troops from Cambodia, the Chinese now floated the possibility of a deal being struck that would lead to power sharing between the CGDK and the Phnom Penh regime. This proposal foundered on the total refusal of the Vietnamese to withdraw and the determination of their Cambodian protégés in Phnom Penh not to accept any arrangement that meant giving up their control of Cambodia's population.

Movement began to take place, slowly, in the following year, 1987. As had been so often the case in Cambodia's history what happened next was as much the result of developments involving stronger external powers as the actions of the contending Cambodians themselves. In 1987 changes taking place in the Soviet Union began to impact on Cambodian affairs. Not only were President Gorbachev's foreign and domestic policies leading to an improvement in relations with the United States and with China, the Soviet Union now began to hint that it was no longer prepared to provide indefinite economic support to Vietnam. At the same time Vietnam began to count the cost of its occupation of Cambodia, a cost that kept rising in terms of the lives of its soldiers and the expense of maintaining them there.

In June 1987 Sihanouk stepped down from his position as the head of the CGDK in order to play a more active role in the search for a settlement. At the end of 1987, and again in early 1988, he had meetings with Hun Sen, the man who had now emerged as the most powerful figure in the Phnom Penh regime. Initially, these meetings did not result in any progress, but the fact that they took place was a reflection of the way in which the broader international scene was changing. This fact was made sharply clear in March 1988 when the Soviet Union failed to offer either material or symbolic aid to Vietnam as Vietnamese and Chinese forces clashed in the Spratly Islands. This lack of Soviet action reminded Vietnam that it could no longer rely on its long-time ally, which was, in any case, pressing Vietnam to withdraw its troops from Cambodia.

From mid-1988 progress towards an eventual settlement of the Cambodia problem took place in fits and starts, a process marked by failed meetings and then by unexpected movements forward. The collapse of communism in Eastern Europe and the dramatic disintegration of the Soviet Union provided the backdrop for the Cambodian endgame.

With their economy in grave difficulties, the Vietnamese leadership came to recognize that some form of accommodation would have to made with China. It was just too large and too strong to ignore, and so reluctantly the Hanoi government withdrew all its troops from Cambodia. But still there was no basis for agreement among the contending Cambodian factions, particularly since the regime in Phnom Penh saw no reason to give up the power it held over most of the country's population. Above all, the Phnom Penh regime refused to countenance the United Nations playing a role in reaching a settlement and its patron, Vietnam, was initially unwilling to press this possibility upon its protégé.

Real movement towards a settlement came in 1991. With Moscow and Peking both anxious to see the Cambodian problem resolved, and with Peking exerting pressure on Vietnam to urge the need for a settlement on the Phnom Penh regime, all Cambodian factions came to accept a United Nations call for a cease-fire in the guerrilla war in May 1991. Then, in June, Sihanouk engineered the breakthrough the international community had been waiting for. He gained the support of all the Cambodian factions, including the regime in Phnom Penh, the State of Cambodia, to meet as a kind of 'super' government in Phnom Penh while the United Nations Transitional Authority in Cambodia (UNTAC) made arrangements for elections to be held in 1993. The detail of these arrangements was incorporated in a peace settlement signed in Paris in October 1991.

The path to the elections held under United Nations' auspices in May 1993 was far from smooth. The Khmer Rouge forces, now operating separately from the former CGDK partners, refused to disarm and made clear that they would not participate in the settlement they had signed. There was widespread political violence, much of it directed against the non-communist opponents of the Phnom Penh regime. And, in January 1993, a bare five months before elections were due to be held, Sihanouk announced that he was ceasing cooperation with UNTAC. His aim was clear. He expected that in the unsettled situation existing in Cambodia the country's political leaders and the international community would call on him to assume a leadership role, perhaps as president of Cambodia before the elections took place. He was, he said, 'ready to exercise power, even if I am called an autocrat'. Never doubting his own indispensability, he claimed that 'People are very upset. They say that only Sihanouk is clean, the only one is Sihanouk. He should be made to come back [from Peking] and take charge of everything.' In the event, the key international backers of the United Nations' plan were not prepared to introduce a new element into an already difficult situation, and when the elections were held Sihanouk, who had returned to Cambodia a day before polling started, was essentially left on the sidelines. There is no doubt that he, like almost everyone else, was surprised at the results that emerged when the elections took place on 23 May 1993.

Contrary to expectations, the Cambodian People's Party (CPP), the party of the regime holding power in Phnom Penh, was beaten into first place by FUNCINPEC (National United Front for an Independent, Peaceful, Neutral and Cooperative Cambodia), the party headed by Sihanouk's son, Prince Ranariddh. (FUNCINPEC gained 45 per cent of the vote to the CPP's 38 per cent.) In an atmosphere of confusion and surprise, and with the CPP suggesting the election result involved fraud, Sihanouk made an unexpected intervention with the aim of immediately returning to a pivotal role in Cambodian politics. He announced that he was forming an interim government in which he would hold the posts of president, prime minister and military commander. Falsely claiming to have the support of Ranariddh, he went on to state that his son and Hun Sen would be his vice-premiers. Within twenty-four hours the prince's gambit had failed. Quite apart from the hesitation of Cambodian politicians to accept these proposals the foreign powers who had worked so hard to bring a Cambodian settlement, and in particular the United States, made clear that Sihanouk could not usurp the election results. For the moment he retired behind the high walls of the royal palace.

Yet Sihanouk still had a role to play. As the CPP made clear that it was not prepared to cede power to FUNCINPEC as the party gaining the largest vote in the May elections, Sihanouk lent his prestige to a compromise arrangement by which there would be a power sharing arrangement between the CPP and FUNCINPEC. Whatever was in-tended at the time, this arrangement effectively left major power in CPP hands, a fact that had long term consequences. But by this stage Sihanouk may not have greatly cared. What was now important to him was a declaration that his loss of power in 1970 was the result of an illegal act. Then, in September 1993, to his great delight Cambodia's constitutional assembly voted to ask him to assume once again the position of King of Cambodia. He was crowned king for a second time on 24 September.

* * * * * *

Cambodia's modern history cannot be written without Sihanouk, though the assertion by the well-known American journalist, Robert Shaplen, that 'Cambodia is Sihanouk' was not true at the time it was made in the 1960s, or at any other time. And what has happened in Cambodia since Sihanouk was once again placed on the throne in 1993 emphasizes this point.

Cambodia since the elections of 1993 has joined those countries, found in many parts of the world, that are dominated by a single party and led by a dominant politician. It is not strictly a 'one party state', for FUNCINPEC continues to exist, as does the Sam Rainsy Party, the party named after its brave but powerless leader. But in all ways that matter Hun Sen and the CPP control Cambodia and in doing so preside over a country that has rightly been described as possessing a 'culture of impunity'. Crimes great and small are committed with an understanding that there is little prospect of prosecution if the perpetrator is linked to the ruling figures in the government.

Put simply, Hun Sen, the former Khmer Rouge military commander who defected to become a Vietnamese protégé and then a leader of the CPP, has seen off all opposition to hold an unchallenged position of power in Cambodia, His shrewd peasant mind has proved more than a match for Prince Ranariddh and Sam Rainsy, men with a Western education but lacking the understanding of brute power possessed by Hun Sen. Any doubts that this was the case were swept away in the events of 1997, first when Sam Rainsy's supporters were killed in a grenade attack while taking part in a protest march and then, later in the year, when a short but bloody confrontation between Hun Sen's and Ranariddh's supporters led to the latter's defeat.

In all of this there has been little place for Sihanouk to exercise power. At best he is able to provide a form of moral leadership, and he can legitimately claim to have brought a reconciliation between Hun Sen and Ranariddh at the end of 1997. There is no doubt that he is revered as selective memories of a 'golden past' have taken root in the minds of many Cambodians. With the horrors of the Pol Pot period still so clearly apparent, the years when Sihanouk was the country's leader have acquired an imagined character that has little to with the actualities of the time. Yet, at the same time, these memories of a better past are squarely recognised as something that cannot be repeated. Cambodians speak of this period as 'Sihanouk time' an era that preceded the awfulness of civil war between 1970 and 1975 and the Pol Pot tyranny that lasted until 1979.

We do not know what Sihanouk thinks of the Cambodia that once again honours him as king. It goes without saying that he deplores the loss of upward of two million of his compatriots while Pol Pot and his associates ruled the country. But we know nothing of his reaction to the culture of impunity, to the reluctance of the Hun Sen government to act against some of the most notorious Khmer Rouge leaders, to the fact that Cambodia shares with Laos the dubious distinction of having the lowest life expectancy in Southeast Asia. He does not speak of the cost that Cambodia is bearing as the result of its HIV-AIDS pandemic.

More than ever was the case until 1970, Sihanouk has become a figurehead for his country, not a man who exercises power. Now in his eighty first year, he has survived beyond the expectations of many, including myself. Indeed, he is surely Southeast Asia's ultimate survivor, not least in recent years in the face of chronic illness. When, in 1993, he said that he wished to be king again he spoke in the following terms: 'I must remain the father of the nation whose task is to re-unite the nation.' He has done his best, but is doubtful if any fair-minded observer would claim that he has achieved that goal.

Cambodia 'after Kampuchea' is a more settled country than it has been for two decades, let alone in the Pol Pot years. But it is a country that continues to face major problems. In closing my postscript for the 1984 edition of this book, I wrote that after Pol Pot Cambodia 'had changed forever'. That comment remains true today. The disturbing truth is that it is still not possible to write about Cambodia's politics without reflecting the fact that there is still little hope that the abuses of the present will give way to a clearly better future.

Milton Osborne
Sydney
February 2004

Correction: In Chapter Seven I refer to Monsignor Tep Im as having attended the Gregorian University in Rome. In fact, he attended the Angelicum, the Pontifical University of St Thomas Aquinas, to give the institution its formal name.

INTRODUCTION

In a Cambodia very different from the shattered country that exists in 1979 many things could drive the kingdom's political leader, Prince Norodom Sihanouk, into towering rage. But nothing was more calculated to do so than a foreign press commentary that referred to Cambodia as 'small'. Cambodia was not 'small' Sihanouk would angrily reply. With a population of seven million and a territory of nearly 70 000 square miles, Cambodia, he insisted, was larger than dozens of other members of the United Nations. The truth was and is, of course, that Cambodia, or Kampuchea as it has been known since 1975, *is* small—small, comparatively weak, and vulnerable to the threats posed by its larger neighbours, especially Vietnam. Whatever the long-term outcome of the dramatic events that brought Cambodia back into the world headlines in early 1979, the fact that a new regime came to power under Vietnamese sponsorship highlights the weakness that has been a fundamental feature of Cambodia's history for more than two centuries.

Although Vietnam is a country whose existence has been deeply imprinted into the consciousness of tens, even hundreds of millions of people throughout the world, the same is scarcely true of Cambodia. Even during the height of the Second Indochina War Cambodia tended to be regarded as a sideshow, an adjunct to events in Vietnam. To the extent that Cambodia was known to the outside world it was in terms of its most remarkable politician, Prince Norodom Sihanouk. The Prince had been King, Chief of State, and Prime Minister of his country. Yet it was seldom his political achievements, or failures, that were emphasised in

9

Western commentary. Rather the press chose to dwell on his other accomplishments. He had been a skilled horseman, a better than amateur musician, a part-time journalist, a lover of good living, rich food, and lovely ladies, and finally a maker of artistically awful feature length films. The Prince had been all these things and the significance of some of these activities reached far into Cambodian politics. The problem was that so little of the foreign commentary that recounted these aspects of Sihanouk's life reflected the deeper and more tragic aspects of Cambodia's present and past.

For the history of Cambodia is deeply tinged with tragedy. The country that today has a population of, perhaps, six million, and may have had a population of over seven million less than a decade ago before a terrible war and subsequently a terrible peace took a staggering toll in human life, was once a mighty power in mainland Southeast Asia. While the Vietnamese were still ruled by China nearly a thousand years ago, and while the Thais had yet to establish their power in the country that today bears their name, the great Cambodian empire with its centre at Angkor was already well-established and set on a path that was to make it one of the greatest states in early Southeast Asian history. At the height of its power in the twelfth and thirteenth centuries Angkorian Cambodia ruled over areas of mainland Southeast Asia that are now parts of Thailand, Laos, and Vietnam. Saigon (Ho Chi Minh City) was once a Cambodian provincial capital. Cambodian princes and great officials ruled over cities in what today is northern Thailand. The power of the ruler at Angkor stretched far to the north up the course of the Mekong River into distant parts of modern Laos.

In this period of Cambodian greatness the mighty temples of Angkor were built that still remain as testimony to human energy and artistic capacity. Scholars think that more than a million people clustered around the great temple complex at Angkor. We know that the capacity of the state to organise and direct manpower was such that the temple of Angkor Wat, probably the largest religious building to be constructed anywhere in the world, was completed in about thirty-five years. Even in the late thirteenth century, a period that historians now call the declining years of Angkorian Cambodia, a proud ambassador from imperial China could still state without hesitation that Angkor was the greatest of the cities in the southern lands.

Yet Angkorian Cambodia was a fragile state and it collapsed under pressure from the growing power of Thailand in the fifteenth century. Once Cambodia's decline began it seemed that it would never halt, for as the centuries passed Cambodia faced the twin threats of stronger neighbours to both the east and west. The Thais has been the people who had brought the Angkorian empire down, but it was the Vietnamese to the east and north of Cambodia who, from the seventeenth century onwards, seemed set on ensuring Cambodia's extinction.

Virtually nothing of this was known in distant Europe, which was scarcely even aware of the magnificent temple ruins that lay hidden in the tropical forests until a French explorer publicised their existence in the middle of the nineteenth century. By that time Cambodia was a vassal of both Thailand and Vietnam and a state whose very existence was in question. During the 1830s Cambodia had undergone the experience of full-scale occupation by the Vietnamese who, like their descendants one hundred and forty years later, established an administration in Phnom Penh composed of 'their' Cambodians. Only agreement between Vietnam and Thailand that Cambodia should survive as a buffer state temporarily staved off what appeared to be the certainty of national disappearance. Cambodia was saved from the probability of extinction by France. Hoping, unrealistically, to find a way into China from Vietnam, France extended colonial control over Cambodia in the 1860s to prevent that weak and scantly populated country falling into the hands of a supposedly hostile, British, rival. The Mekong River ran through Cambodia and it was up the Mekong that the French, initially, saw their road into China as lying. The Mekong very shortly proved to be no commercial route into China but the French remained in Cambodia.

The fact that it was the French who were the colonial masters in Cambodia partly explains why the country was so little known even in the mid-twentieth century. There was foreign awareness of French Indochina, but little realisation that this term encompassed Vietnam, Cambodia, and the various states that were linked together to form modern Laos. The European nations had held highly parochial views of their colonies. So it was that the British knew of developments in India, the Dutch of the problems associated with Indonesia, while the French were preoccupied with what they called 'Our Indochina'. For the most part, however, there was little interest in the colonial possessions of other countries. And when the First Indochina War did draw attention to that part of the world such interest as there was concentrated on the major actions fought in Vietnam. Since they were relatively less important in military terms little interest was accorded Cambodia or Laos. It was all too easy in the 1950s to have had a reasonable education but to be profoundly ignorant of Cambodia —a fact that I have good reason to remember.

In 1958 I learnt to my considerable surprise that I was to be posted to the Australian mission in Phnom Penh, Cambodia's capital. Still dazed at the news of this unexpected posting, I was congratulated by an older colleague for the opportunity it would give me to visit Angkor. I was saved from eternal shame by failing to respond, 'Angkor what?' I made the best of whatever small diplomatic skills I possessed to pretend that I knew all about Angkor as I made my way rapidly to the departmental library to consult an encyclopaedia.

This was the beginning of an association with Cambodia that has continued for twenty years. Over that period I have lived in Cambodia for two extended periods and visited the country on many occasions. I have remained continuously fascinated by the study of its history and politics, whether this has involved travelling through the country itself, poring over dusty archives in Paris and Phnom Penh, or peering at microfilmed newspapers in libraries in Ithaca, New York, or Melbourne. With sadness I have seen an apparently gay and untroubled Southeast Asian state change over the years until, with the end of the war in April 1975, a new and fiercely radical regime took power in Phnom Penh which sought to totally transform the country. A few outside observers saw Pol Pot's Kampuchea as a revolutionary model to be admired. A rather larger number took a different point of view, believing that whatever the difficulties in arriving at precise figures something terrible had happened after April 1975. I was one of this latter group. I am uncertain about magnitudes and sceptical about some of the accounts of internal developments in Kampuchea after the Pol Pot regime came to power. Despite these reservations, however, I believe that both as the result of deliberate policy and through developments over which the Kampuchean Communist leaders had no control, the population in a country that had suffered so much in the closing years of the Second Indochina War continued to suffer terribly in the years of 'peace'. In 1979 the population suffers again as it becomes part of a new war following Vietnam's decision to establish its Cambodian protégés as the government in Phnom Penh.

But this is not a book about developments since 1975. Instead it is a book that seeks to indicate some answers to the questions that must repeatedly be in the mind of anyone who thought he or she 'knew' Cambodia before the fighting began. Why and how did it happen? I look for some answers by examining the year 1966, a year that I judge to have been a turning point in Cambodia's modern history. In 1966 I returned to Cambodia after an absence of nearly five years. As a Cornell graduate student I was studying the impact of French rule in Cambodia during the nineteenth century. My principal concern was those political developments involving Prince Norodom Sihanouk's great grandfather, Norodom I, who had fought a lonely, bitter, and ultimately unsuccessful battle to preserve the right to rule Cambodia rather than to see that rule pass into the hands of the French.

Despite these historical preoccupations I could not ignore the contemporary political scene that was the concern of Phnom Penh's constantly grinding rumour mill. I kept a journal that is the basis for much of the material that follows in this book. It is not the only basis. Whatever understanding I had of political developments in 1966 was partly founded upon lessons I had learnt about Cambodia during the more than two years I worked in the chancery building on the Boulevard Norodom under the guidance of a head of mission who was a notably able political reporter. Moreover, greater understanding has come with the passage of time. The events that did not always make sense in 1966 have acquired both sense and clarity when viewed in perspective. What follows is a partial record of a vital year, a year during which Cambodia, its leaders, and its population became increasingly locked into a steady slide towards disaster.

Milton Osborne

April 1979

CHAPTER ONE

Cambodia 1966

When I landed at Phnom Penh's Pochentong airport it was almost seven years to the day since I had first stepped onto the baking concrete. It was early April, the worst month of the Cambodian year when the temperature regularly rises above the century, the humidity is overwhelming but the cooling rains of the monsoon are still at least a month away. Phnom Penh in 1966 was a very different place from what it had been in 1959, and I had a very different status. For nearly two and a half years between 1959–61 I had enjoyed the privileges and pleasures of serving as a junior member of the Australian Embassy at a time when Phnom Penh, for a foreigner, was an attractive, even gay city. If the charm of the city was provincial, there was charm nonetheless. Just how 'provincial' the city was in French terms I was not to realise until years later when I saw in southern France the models for the Post Office Square, the bars and cafés, the Magasin Modern that just occasionally had in stock the items one wanted to buy, and the villas of the French Quarter with their gravelled courtyards behind walls topped with iron spikes and bougainvillaea.

We foreigners felt provincial in other ways too. A visit to Saigon or Bangkok not only involved translation to bigger and more modern cities it also seemed to emphasise the 'provincial' quality of Phnom Penh's politics. It appeared that politics in Thailand and southern Vietnam were 'serious' in a way that the princely politics of Sihanouk's Cambodia were not. This was an error of judgment that many of us made. Even those who were wiser could not wholly disregard those aspects of Sihanouk's behaviour that sometimes seemed to place as much importance on leading a dance band in performances of his own music as on the dull business of running the country. Appropriated as members of his court, foreign diplomats found themselves prisoners of an insomniac prince who at midnight laughingly assured them that they could leave the party but that he would be playing his music until dawn. As they danced under the stars inside the royal palace grounds the foreigners pretended to ignore the fact that the lavatories could not be flushed until, at nearly three in the morning, the city's fire engines arrived to replenish the water supplies.

A great deal had happened between my leaving Phnom Penh in 1961 and returning in 1966. Just how serious 'politics' were in neighbouring Vietnam was now only too clear and Saigon retained only a vestige of its former glamour. Cambodia still had a provincial quality, but now it was an austere place by comparison with the city I had left five years before. The centre of the city still preserved its Gallic architectural charm, but there were many more squatters' shacks on the outskirts. Sihanouk's determination to preserve Cambodia's national integrity had led him to proclaim a series of economic reforms involving nationalisation and the rejection of American aid, and to sever relations with America. Some of the effects of these policies were immediately apparent to a visitor who had known Phnom Penh in other days. There were fewer cars and foreigners in the streets. Many of the bars and restaurants that had catered to the foreign community six or seven years before had gone, as had the foreign banks and agency houses.

These changes were the obvious ones. There were other much less obvious changes and it took me some time to understand that politics now were a serious matter in Cambodia. What had so often been hidden from view six or seven years before could now be seen, even by a foreigner. This fact alone made Cambodia in 1966 a country of extraordinary interest and one in which a surprisingly large number of persons were ready to talk frankly about their hopes and fears for the future. Whether they perceived the fact clearly or otherwise, Cambodians were aware that their country was in the midst of great change. What had seemed to be certainties in the past were no longer so. The apparently clear-cut answers to the country's problems that had been offered by

Sihanouk since he had successfully gained independence from France in 1953 and then succeeded in dominating the kingdom's politics after 1955 no longer seemed to serve the changed conditions of the times. Quite suddenly so much that was dangerous and threatening in Cambodian society could no longer be ignored or glossed over. With the help of Cambodian friends and as the result of dozens of chance conversations I came to understand how fragile Cambodia was in 1966; fragile and diseased.

The disease was corruption, a pervasive corruption of values, of political morals, and of purpose. Some men and women were not corrupt; some on the political right and some on the political left. But they were the exceptions. It is of course the elite I am writing about. The further down the social scale a man or woman was placed, the less were the opportunities to share in corruption. But this did not prevent the city and country poor from being touched by corruption. When I made my last visit to Cambodia in 1971 the effects of wartime corruption were apparent in the capital and in the provincial centres it was still possible to visit. Long before that time the lot of the peasant in some areas of Cambodia had come close to being intolerable as he and his family laboured at the base of a corrupt pyramid of usury, bribery, and influence. In the capital the existence of poverty was widely known in 1966 but largely hidden in the back lanes and shanty towns that were avoided by both foreigners and prosperous Cambodians alike.

While Cambodia's recent history has been filled with tragedy this does not mean that it is totally without humour. Perhaps what has changed as I look back at certain events is that the apparent comedy of 1966 has now assumed a 'black' character. With the passage of time I can now see that there was little, superficially humourous or otherwise, that was not deeply offensive to those who chose a left-wing solution for their country. And the same perspective stresses how totally incapable the men of the right were of seeing that their political choice left them no other exit except disaster.

A final polarisation between left and right took place in Cambodia in 1966 with an extraordinary range of developments, some important some trivial. The events of this year, I believe, convinced many on the left that there was no alternative to revolution while they planted the thought ever more firmly in the minds of the right that sooner or later Sihanouk would have to go. Now that I realise this was so, I understand more fully the atmosphere of barely averted crisis that was so clearly present in Phnom Penh in 1966. I think I now understand why there was an almost frenetic interest in such matters as the curious case of the Kep casino. I certainly understand better the desperation and frustration felt by holders of high school diplomas who could not get jobs. And I can see why an acquaintance who was a member of one of Cambodia's most distinguished official families could, in his own terms, see no other way to achieve change short of revolution. Yet even before I came to these later perceptions, to live in Cambodia in 1966 was to sense that great change was coming and while I feared whatever lay ahead, the present gave scant cause for optimism.

CHAPTER TWO

The Curious Case of the Kep Casino

It once was the case that Cambodians loved to gamble. To do so was illegal, unless the gambling involved was the state-sponsored national lottery. But never was such a law so widely breached, except perhaps in Australia's Broken Hill. Australians are said to be such inveterate gamblers that they will bet on which of two flies will crawl more quickly across a window plane. In Phnom Penh Cambodians and Chinese alike gambled on the exact moment it would rain each day during the rainy season. Whether they won or lost depended on the city's Chinese gambling 'king' for it was he who decreed when the rain had indeed begun to fall. The 'king' was a man of power whose wealth and organisation would have been the envy of the bosses running the numbers racket in Harlem.

Old and young, rich and poor gambled. A sign of Prince Sihanouk's displeasure with an aunt, uncle, nephew, niece, or cousin from the large and frequently self-indulgent Cambodian royal family would be revealed in a newspaper announcement that 'a highness' or even a 'royal highness' had been 'seized during a police descent upon an illegal gambling game'. This did not happen often and such other arrests as were made reflected less the government's determination to suppress small scale private gambling than the individual's failure to calculate the proper bribe to pay the police. Even where gambling was on a larger scale there were never any hints that the gambling 'king' faced the prospect of arrest, let alone a fine or imprisonment, for his organisation clearly knew where payments needed to be made. In

Phnom Penh, in any case, gambling had patrons at a high level. Sihanouk's mother, Queen Kossamak, was far too shrewd a business woman to ignore the potential offered by renting out some of her property as gambling places. There were wry jokes as to whether she got a better return from this use of her real estate or from the property she rented to the brothel keepers.

For years there had been one period of the year when gambling was permitted to take place publicly without any attempt at concealment. This was at Chaul Chhnam, the Cambodian New Year that fell, in Western terms, in early April. For four or five days the legal restraints on gambling were removed and the streets of Phnom Penh's Chinese quarter were thronged with eager players testing their skill and luck in a wide range of games of chance. The skills the gamblers displayed scarcely argued for their confining this activity to one short period of the year. Although the open gambling over Chaul Chhnam enjoyed the blessing of tradition, it scarcely provided the opportunities desired by serious gamblers, nor did it swell the revenues of the state. To meet these needs Sihanouk and his advisers devised a splendidly Cambodian compromise. They would open two casinos, one at Bokor on a plateau overlooking the Gulf of Thailand and the other on the gulf itself at the small resort town of Kep. These casinos would be open only to foreigners, in effect to the Chinese resident in Cambodia whose passion for gambling was possibly even greater than that of the Cambodians themselves. With these casinos open, the policy planners appear to have concluded that the gamblers in the Chinese community would be happy and that the state would have a steady additional source of revenue.

There was one more calculation. Located more than one hundred miles from the capital the casinos would not be under the public scrutiny they would sustain in Phnom Penh. Since this was so no one need bother too much that Cambodians broke the rules that said they should not enter the casinos to gamble. Indeed, no one did bother very much and the Phnom Penh elite streamed to Kep to play at fan tan and roulette. They streamed to Kep but not to Bokor since for much of the time this magnificent site, which must be reached by a winding road rising from sea level to over three thousand feet, is shrouded in thick cloud and mist. Bokor, moreover, had an association with death ever since the

Vietminh had attacked the hotel during the First Indochinese War and that was scarcely a memory conducive to the lighthearted loss and gain of money.

So it was that until June 1966 the Kep casino continued to flourish despite a deteriorating economic situation that caused Sihanouk to make increasingly frequent public expressions of concern and led him to speak of the possibility of introducing a 'Communist economy'. But in early June the Kep casino closed forever. In the first weekend of that month with the usual influx of visitors from Phnom Penh the frenetic but ordered business of gambling was suddenly ended by the arrival of a gang of thugs who proceeded to smash all that could be smashed.

Windows, mirrors, furniture and fixtures, all were smashed and destroyed with a thoroughness that impressed those who saw the process taking place or the results once the gang had left. The Chinese businessman who held the concession for the casino was said to be distraught, allowing emotion to overcome his usual measured calm. Meanwhile, although the sacking of the casino had not been reported in the Phnom Penh newspapers, the knowledgeable inhabitants of the city began to discuss the affair. Surely, ran the first estimations, the holder of the concession had failed to pay a sufficient amount of money to the local police chief. Such a failure—surprising in a man of the concessionaire's reputation—could almost certainly be expected to lead to harassment from those authorities who would expect to benefit from regular bribes.

The thoughtful assessors of rumours, an almost full-time profession in Phnom Penh, were unsatisfied by this explanation. That there should have been police harassment was to be expected if the concessionaire had indeed failed to make his clandestine payments in the appropriate fashion. But to destroy the casino, that seemed to be carrying things too far. Now the local police would have no basis on which to demand their bribes. Without a casino how could they be rewarded for providing protection? There had to be another explanation. There was, and the men and women who daily weighed and assessed gossip and rumour were delighted when their doubts about the first and most obvious explanation for the curious affair were shown to be justified. Less than a week after the Kep casino had been sacked the 'true' story was making the rounds. It had not been the police who had so thoroughly destroyed the casino. It had, of course, been the casino concessionaire himself!

The new story linked the casino at Kep with a 'high personality' in Phnom Penh. With the press still muzzled the rumours went no further in identification, but the role and interests of the high personality were clear enough. In order to ensure that he could run his casino in Kep the Chinese concessionaire had to pay a monthly bribe to the high personality in Phnom Penh of no less than forty thousand American dollars. This the concessionaire had been prepared to do. But then it seemed the high personality wanted more. The concessionaire said no. The high personality threatened police harassment. The concessionaire arranged the destruction of his casino.

A curious case it seemed, but scarcely a matter involving politics. Such an estimation was shown to be wrong when two weeks after the casino had been sacked no less a person than the Minister for Internal Security, Kou Roun, made public a report on the affair. It confirmed the basic facts that had been the subject of so much Phnom Penh gossip. The concessionaire had been responsible for the destruction of the casino. But the official version of why he had acted in this way was rather different. The concessionaire, Kou Roun asserted, destroyed the casino because he had learnt that the authorities were going to enforce the law that banned Cambodians from gambling. There was no hint that a 'high personality' had been squeezing the concessionaire for forty thousand American dollars a month and trying to squeeze him for more.

There was, however, another curious revelation. Kou Roun stated that Chau Seng, the head of Prince Sihanouk's private secretariat, had taken the unusual step of presenting directly to Sihanouk a report, prepared by the concessionaire himself, on the sacking of the Kep Casino. Chau Seng had done this because he could not resist the pressure placed upon him by a 'high feminine bourgeois personality of the capital'. What, the Phnom Penh elite asked themselves, was one to make of this?

To understand the interest generated by Kou Roun's association with the affair and his clearly critical references to Chau Seng it is necessary to know something of the two men. Anyone searching for two men of contrasting personality within Sihanouk's Cambodia in the 1960s would have had to look hard to find a more striking example than that provided by Kou Roun and Chau Seng. The former was a thickset man whose hard face and gruff manner seemed appropriate to his task as head of Sihanouk's security forces. Among those with a French education he was known as *le bourreau*, the executioner, a nickname aptly chosen for the man who presided over the sudden imprisonments of suspected leftists—something that had become more and more of a feature of the security forces' activities—and who authorised their 'questioning' in the cells that stood not far from the capital's central market. It was a sign of the times in the Phnom Penh of 1966 that one's acquaintances could all readily say where suspects were taken to be beaten, and worse.

Kou Roun belonged to the 'old school'. He had been one of Sihanouk's close associates even before the Prince had abdicated the throne to lead his own political party. This made him part of the older political generation by the middle of the 1960s. And he was of an older generation in terms of the ideas he had for solving problems. I once asked him how the government was coping with the existence within Cambodia's borders of significant indigenous ethnic minorities, the varied hill peoples lumped into such an undifferentiated mass and called *montagnards* by the French, a term that was taken over by the Americans during their war in Vietnam. There was no problem, Kou Roun assured me; 'We Khmerise them.' Just what this meant I was to learn later when reports trickled down from the distant hills that told of the Cambodian authorities acting towards their minorities with all the disdain and despite of the worst colonial regimes. Nomadic groups were forced into fixed settlements and failure to comply brought harsh physical punishment. When rebellion began against Sihanouk's government in the late 1960s many of the varied hill peoples joined with those who opposed Phnom Penh.

Not all of the old school were as humourless or so brutal as Kou Roun. Few were untouched by avarice, but none, surely, were more avaricious. He set an example that was much copied by his men. He was disliked and he was feared. The fact of being disliked was one of the two things that Kou Roun shared with Chau Seng, that and avarice. But it is hard to think of anything else that the two men had in common. Chau Seng was a self-proclaimed progressive, a man who ultimately had to flee Sihanouk's Cambodia and who became an active advocate for the cause of the left-wing forces fighting against the Lon Nol regime from 1970 to 1975. Since the Communist victory he has not chosen to return to his country.

No one has ever explained very satisfactorily how Chau Seng managed to survive in Cambodia's politics as long as he did. He is an able man who first came to Sihanouk's attention when he returned from France in the fifties and on his own initiative prepared a report on the problems of secondary education in Cambodia. But with his intelligence goes a seemingly inexhaustable capacity to irritate, annoy, and offend others. How was it then, many have asked, that Chau Seng not only repeatedly held important government positions under Sihanouk but managed to become head of the Prince's own private secretariat? I think the answer lies in the extent to which Chau Seng's role as the *enfant terrible* of Cambodian politics had an almost irresistible appeal to Sihanouk. Time and again Sihanouk told his listeners that if he had not been born a prince he would have been a man of the left. And here was Chau Seng who boldly proclaimed his progressive views. Though he sometimes expressed his contempt for intellectuals the Prince was secretly rather envious of those who could claim such a description, as Chau Seng certainly could. Chau Seng never hid his dislike of 'imperialists'. There were many times when Sihanouk did not hide his dislike for this group either, but there were other times when he had to temper his feelings with a discretion that Chau Seng cheerfully refused to show. In short Chau Seng was many of the things that Sihanouk at times wished to be. He was also intelligent and hard working.

Like Kou Roun, Chau Seng was a man who desired wealth. He found his progressive views no barrier to the acquisition of real estate in Phnom Penh and a rubber plantation in the provinces. Whether this reflected a shrewd assessment that in order to continue in political life he would need to have funds behind him or whether it was merely a reflection of a personal double standard is unclear. Certainly the real left despised him just as much as the men and women of the right disliked him, that is to say, intensely.

To have these two men apparently involved on opposite sides of a public scandal was of the greatest interest to the avid observers of political in-fighting in Phnom Penh. But the affair remained a puzzle nonetheless. Presuming that there *had* been a high personality in Phnom Penh who had demanded and received $40 000 per month from the Kep casino's concessionaire, who could this be? And who was the high bourgeois feminine personality of the capital who, if Kou Roun was correct, had prevailed on Chau Seng to transmit a report from the concessionaire direct to Sihanouk? Could it be that the two high personalities were one and the same person? And why should Sihanouk be interested in a squalid gambling scandal in any event?

Just who the high personalities were was never revealed, not even to the most inquisitive foreigner. The likelihood seems very strong that the high bourgeois feminine personality was either Prince Sihanouk's consort Monique, a commoner and not a princess like Sihanouk's other wife, or her mother. It would by no means have been impossible that one of the corrupt clique that gathered around Monique had indeed been involved in the arrangement that called for the monthly payment of $40 000. To a considerable extent, however, the identities of these figures does not matter for an understanding of the deeper significance of the affair. This significance does not lie simply in the evidence it provided of the widespread presence of corruption. This was certainly important and undoubtedly represented an affront to the views of those leftist politicians such as Khieu Samphan who were still weighing in their minds what course of action they should follow. Just as important, however, was the way in which the curious case of the Kep casino reflected the deeper pattern of Cambodian politics. This pattern was one in which although neither the right nor the left in Cambodia's overt politics yet felt able to challenge Sihanouk's paramountcy they would seize any chance to try to make political capital out of events and developments that did not seem to have immediate political significance.

The increasing polarisation of politics in 1966 led to this situation, but there was still a reluctance in the world of open politics to go beyond the step of seeking political advantage to that much more fateful step of seeking to act without Sihanouk's approval or against his wishes. Many of the right would not have worried much, if at all, about the fact of corruption associated with a casino, but they saw the events at Kep as yet further evidence of the decline of the state under Sihanouk's wilful rule. The left's sense of political morality did lead them to worry about corruption and the reflection of this provided by the affair at Kep, but like the right they too looked at the deeper significance. How could a state be transformed and iniquities removed without a revolution to purge such practices and those associated with them from the body politic. Without the slightest doubt they saw Chau Seng's role in the affair as a clear revelation of that man's weakness and lack of true revolutionary commitment.

As for Sihanouk, there would be little question that it was his intervention that brought the Kep affair to an end for suddenly the disclosures ceased. This as much as anything else points to members of his wife's family having some involvement. Sihanouk, until his deposition in 1970, could never bring himself to act firmly to curb Monique and her clique from increasingly flagrant corruption. But he would act to silence those who sought to make public attacks upon them.

It might have seemed that the events associated with the destruction of the Kep casino would have provided a lesson of some sort to Sihanouk, a warning that gambling in Cambodia carried with it risks that could involve politics. Three years later, in 1969, the Prince decided to open another casino, but this time in Phnom Penh and one that was open to all, foreigner and Cambodian alike. It would be dangerous to give excessive emphasis to the political implications of this decision. Nevertheless there is no doubt that in the circumstances of continuing economic decline and increasing internal and external threat to his regime in Phnom Penh, Sihanouk's decision was seen as yet one further indication of his inability to order the affairs of state with both sense and dignity. And this reinforced the decision of the right-wing to depose him. By 1969 the Prince was even more a prisoner of his whims than he had been before, most particularly he was devoting even more time to the film making that was suddenly revealed in 1966 as his consuming passion.

CHAPTER THREE

A Border Incident

If the events associated with the sacking of the Kep casino provided a topic for Phnom Penh elite gossips to mix scandal with politics, other events in 1966 had a serious character and are probably correctly judged as having had broad national implications. Nowhere was this more true than in the case of the incidents involving Cambodia's borders with its western and eastern neighbours. The open hostilities that developed between Kampuchea and a united Vietnam and led in January 1979 to the overthrow of the Pol Pot regime and Vietnamese occupation of the country in support of their Cambodian clients have underlined a fundamentally important theme in Cambodia's history. It is a theme that has been reinforced throughout the centuries since Vietnamese settlers started advancing into what had previously been Cambodian lands in the Mekong River delta. For Cambodians of all political persuasions the Vietnamese have never been less than a threat and frequently have been a dangerous enemy.

The pressures that bore upon Cambodia in the middle 1960s did not change this fundamental theme, however much the range of competing and conflicting factors provided qualifications of one sort or another. An expert writer of that type of literate novel of politics and espionage which intertwines successive bizarre or unexpected plots to produce a credible whole could hardly improve upon the elements involved in the politics of Cambodia's borders. I doubt if the catalogue that follows comes anywhere near completeness. During 1966 Sihanouk's government was engaged

in negotiations with the Vietnamese Communists—the representatives of the Democratic Republic of Vietnam from Hanoi and
those of the southern National Liberation Front—for a border
agreement that would recognise Cambodia's existing boundaries.
The Vietnamese Communists with Sihanouk's at least tacit
agreement were using sections of northeastern Cambodia for the
shipment of supplies to their troops fighting the Americans and
the forces of the Saigon regime in southern Vietnam. Some areas
of the border were used by Vietnamese Communists as resting
and staging points for their troops, again with some Cambodian
connivance. But while this was happening Sihanouk was making
hesitant approaches to the United States with the hope that the
Americans, should developments in Vietnam turn out differently
from what he expected, would restrain their Vietnamese allies from
seeking to gain territory at Cambodia's expense.

Accompanying this situation was a large-scale illicit trade
backwards and forwards across the border with Vietnam. A rather
different weekend outing from Phnom Penh took the form of
driving down to those border points with Vietnam where smuggled
goods were on open sale. American military equipment of all sorts
could be bought, including weapons I was told, if one knew the
right man to ask and had the necessary cash in dollars, of course,
not in Cambodian riels. Sometimes these visits to the black markets
of the border zones were enlivened by the reality of the war in
Vietnam making its presence very apparent. Such was the case
one day when I was at Phnom Den in the extreme southeast of
Cambodia. There in the fabled Seven Mountains area I joined
the traders to watch with a curiously detached fascination an F-105
drop its bombs a bare half mile away, the blast and concussion
making all too apparent what the difference between war in
Vietnam and the lack of it in Cambodia really meant.

Phnom Den, and the much larger black market at Bavet in the
extreme east of the so-called Parrot's Beak region—it was known
as the Duck's Bill in French times and I have never understood
why there should have been this ornithological transmogrification
—were remarkable for the variety of goods they could supply. The
variety included Australian whiskey which, I remember, a kind
Cambodian host mistakenly thought that as an Australian I would
prefer to Scotch and laid in a supply when I visited him. But

however wide the variety of goods and whatever the fascination of the clandestine economic processes involved, these markets with their open display of stolen or smuggled goods were minor affairs compared with the really important traffic across the borders. This was the traffic in rice and other essential supplies that passed from Cambodia into Vietnam as enterprising Cambodian merchants supplied what the Vietnamese Communists needed and the Cambodian army officers who controlled the traffic grew rich on the bribes they received to permit it to exist. The going rate for the bribe necessary to have a Cambodian army officer permit a truck to pass through the area under his command and across the border was one thousand five hundred American dollars. This was the price for each vehicle and convoys of ten or more vehicles were said to be common.

So the border held many opportunities and many risks. The risks were particularly high for those peasant farmers whose villages lay near the border, for not only was there disagreement between Cambodia and the Saigon regime as to just where the border lay, but the nature of the war being fought in southern Vietnam ensured that from time to time the conflict spilled over into Cambodia. The story of one such incident, or more exactly a linked pair of incidents, gives a sense of the problems and tensions present in Cambodia in 1966 whenever the border was involved.

On 31 July 1966 a sizeable Cambodian village near the Cambodian–Vietnamese border was attacked by United States helicopters. The village was named Thlok Trach and a pregnant Cambodian woman was killed during the attack. Public reaction in Phnom Penh, led by Sihanouk, was immediate and bitter. For Sihanouk in particular the incident could not have come at a worse time. He was slowly seeking to change the thrust of his foreign policy and giving clear hints that he did not rule out the possibility of a *rapprochement* with the United States. He had gone as far as inviting Averell Harriman to visit Cambodia in September and an incident such as this threw the possibility of such a visit into question. This was only one consideration. Seeing the Americans fighting in Vietnam as allies of Cambodia's long-time enemies, the Vietnamese, the attack was instantly slotted into Cambodian minds and evoked again the deep fear of Vietnamese aggression. And then there was the basic futility of the attack. Thlok Trach, the Cambodians insisted, was no staging point for troops. It had no military associations. It was simply a village in which a pregnant Cambodian woman was now dead.

Three days after the attack a convoy of foreigners was taken from Phnom Penh to view the village. The service and press attachés from the various foreign missions in Phnom Penh travelled eastwards to the border and Thlok Trach. No sooner had they arrived than a further attack on an area near the village began, this time by American jet aircraft. The various attachés and their Cambodian guides huddled behind trees and in ditches while the American aircraft made several runs over the village, then retreated. On this second occasion two small children were drowned when they fell into a watercourse while running from the attack.

If Sihanouk had been bitterly angry following the first attack he was to become after the second attack quite literally speechless with rage. After a delay of nearly ten days a United States statement on the incidents was issued in both Washington and Saigon. The statement expressed regret for the deaths of civilians but noted in an uncompromising fashion that the village concerned was not shown on the latest maps available to the United States forces to be in Cambodia. When Sihanouk gave a news conference on 13 August, he was in a state of high emotion. Speaking in French, his statements and responses were constantly interrupted by his own nearly hysterical laughter. Several times he was so overcome with feeling that he was unable to finish a sentence, so that as I listened to the radio I heard one of Sihanouk's French journalists, Jean Barré, finding the words for him. The Harriman visit was cancelled, Sihanouk told his listeners, for what the United States was doing by claiming that the village was not in Cambodian territory was to rob the country of its land. This was, he said, 'worse than a declaration of war.'

In speaking as he did Sihanouk was only giving vent, in his inimitable fashion, to a widespread feeling in the capital. How could the United States take the position it did when the Cambodians themselves relied on United States Army Mapping Service maps printed in 1964 to define their country's borders?

It was these maps, the Cambodians insisted, that showed the village was in Cambodia. Even right-wing Cambodians who had hoped that Sihanouk would go ahead with his plans to seek a more amicable relationship with the United States began to wonder whether there might not be some truth in the point of view being offered by Chau Seng's newspaper *La Dépêche*. There the argument presented was that the two attacks were an effort by the United States military to sabotage Sihanouk's initiative in inviting Harriman to Phnom Penh. The fact that *La Dépêche* opposed improved relations with the United States was conveniently not mentioned at this stage.

Five days after Sihanouk's press conference there was a further United States statement on the incidents and this was given wide coverage by the Cambodians. The United States now agreed that the village that had been attacked was under Cambodian administration, but insistence was still placed on the village being inside Vietnamese territory. The following day, 19 August 1966, Sihanouk gave another press conference. It involved a strange shift in position. Thlok Trach, said Sihanouk, is located in an area where United States maps show the border to be 'undefined'. Since Cambodia administers the villages in this area, then by international legal standards, Sihanouk asserted, the villages are in Cambodia. In the days that followed it became clear that the incidents at Thlok Trach were not to dominate the news any further. It took some time before I could find out what had happened. The story was never made public.

When the two incidents occurred the Headquarters of the Cambodian Army supplied a map reference for the location of Thlok Trach. This map reference placed Thlok Trach clearly within Cambodia's border on the 1 to 250 000 map of the area. The service and press attachés who went to see Thlok Trach on 3 August did not have an opportunity to check the map reference they had been given since the jet attack began almost as soon as they arrived. Why had Sihanouk suddenly shifted from talking of the village being in Cambodia to its being under Cambodian administration? The key to this change lay in the existence of other maps and, even more important, in the fact that the map reference supplied by the Cambodian Army was wrong. The larger scale, 1 to 50 000, United States maps did indeed show the area in which

Thlok Trach was located as having an undefined border between Cambodia and Vietnam. The new, corrected map reference that the Cambodian Army now provided placed the village well inside Vietnamese territory according to the maps drawn up by the former Service Géographique de l'Indochine during the final stages of French colonial control. Faced with these facts the shift was made from stressing location to sovereignty through administration. Later inquiries at Army Headquarters brought a denial that the first and incorrect map reference had ever been given.

The incidents connected with Thlok Trach can be viewed in many ways. By comparison with the carnage of war that was part of Vietnam's fate in 1966 the events in Thlok Trach were a minor affair, though they would never be viewed in those terms by those whose relatives had been killed and houses destroyed. Again, if comparison is taken as the yardstick, the killing and destruction that took place in Cambodia itself after Sihanouk's overthrow made such an affair appear insignificant. The real importance of the Cambodian reaction to the Thlok Trach attacks is probably to be found less in discussion of death and destruction than in terms of what these meant as a reflection of the Cambodians' deep concern that their country might not survive as an independent state.

By 1966 there was not only a polarisation in Cambodia's political life but there was also a new readiness for men to do what would have been impossible five or six years before. They were prepared to talk of Sihanouk's disappearance from the political scene, even to a foreigner. With this mood abroad one of the obvious questions that sprang to mind was, 'How had Sihanouk survived so long?' No single answer to this question is satisfactory, but there is no doubt that part of the answer lies in the incontestable fact that Sihanouk in his foreign policy was dedicated to preserving Cambodia intact. Some of the policies he followed in pursuit of this goal may have been dubious in the eyes of both his critics and his supporters. But that he was in this a 'true Cambodian' was beyond dispute.

In terms of Cambodia's historical experience there was good reason to fear that the country might, at some future date, cease to exist. The Vietnamese had occupied Cambodia in the 1830s and tried to turn it into a copy of their own country. The arrival of the French as colonialists in the 1860s may well have prevented Cambodia from falling under joint occupation by Thailand and Vietnam. As recently as the Second World War Thailand had reoccupied the northwestern provinces of Battambang and Siemreap that had been under Thai control throughout the nineteenth century. Foreign commentators might see Sihanouk as 'obsessed' with threats from his neighbours but in this Sihanouk was essentially reflecting the feelings of the people. The attacks upon Thlok Trach, followed by American insistence that the village was not in Cambodia, were not just an affront to Cambodian sovereignty; they were a reminder that a country of perhaps seven million people which lies between two states with populations many times that number is indeed a fragile country.

If Sihanouk was deeply concerned to preserve his country from further reduction in size, how could he agree to the supply of rice to the Vietnamese Communists whom he saw as ultimately more dangerous to Cambodia than the American-supported regime in Saigon? And what of the army officers who grew rich by permitting large-scale smuggling across the border, again to benefit the Communists as well as themselves? To seek strictly logical and consistent answers in the frequently less than logical and often inconsistent world of Cambodian politics in 1966 is unrewarding. Sihanouk sought to play one side against another; to open talks with the Americans while negotiating with the Vietnamese Communists, to hedge his bets since he knew he was playing from a position of weakness rather than strength. As for the army officers locked into the smuggling trade, there is no reason to believe that they any less than Sihanouk feared what might happen if the Vietnamese Communists should win the war in Vietnam. But they, like so many others in Cambodia, had come to regard illegal profit as not only attractive but indeed essential. In an army that was underpaid and poorly supplied it was not hard to think in these terms. And as men of the right they had the fatal rightist's flaw of failing to think beyond the immediate present and immediate gain.

The fear of war spilling over the borders of Cambodia continued to haunt Cambodians up to the time when the right mounted their successful coup against Sihanouk in 1970. In a mis-estimation of profound proportions the leaders of that coup, Lon Nol, Sirik Matak, Son Ngoc Thanh, and others appear to have sincerely believed that by removing Sihanouk they would, among other things, ensure Cambodia's territorial survival. In a dramatically paradoxical fashion they played their parts in bringing about the situation that developed after April 1975 in which the new Communist masters of Kampuchea fought against the 'fraternal' Communists of Vietnam. As fighting intensified throughout 1978 the rhetoric that came from Phnom Penh was coloured by the ideology of Kampuchea's Communists leaders. But so far as Vietnam was concerned the message was the same as that of Sihanouk's Cambodia. Vietnam was the enemy. Vietnam sought to conquer Kampuchea. Vietnam would not succeed. But the Vietnamese did and the nightmare vision shared by Sihanouk and his countrymen became a shattering reality.

CHAPTER FOUR

Le Far Ouest

'I have decided', I said to my princely friend, 'to visit Pailin.' There were a great many princes in Cambodia in 1966 and to know one did not represent any particular social achievement. But knowing this particular prince did mean a great deal to me personally. We had met first in 1960 and the friendship that began then was both real and lasting. It has also given me an extraordinary range of insights into Cambodian and most particularly Phnom Penh society. As the great great grandson of King Sisowath, who had reigned from 1904 to 1927, this prince was a member of the Sisowath branch of the Cambodian royal family, the rivals of the Norodom branch to which Sihanouk belonged. In a fundamental sense he was apolitical and incorruptible. Perhaps he did hide behind a playboy's manner, and, at times, a playboy's behaviour, but he had a lively intelligence and a shrewd estimate of the strengths and weaknesses of Cambodian politicians of every political hue. He was both close enough to royal family intrigues and yet far enough removed from any possibility of playing a role in them to provide devastatingly detailed accounts of royal folly and excess. He knew people everywhere and I felt sure that he would know someone in Battambang city from where I would have to begin my travel to Pailin.

Now, as we sat drinking a mid-morning beer in the Nouveau Tricotin restaurant, a Chinese restaurant despite its name, this prince looked at me with amazement. I felt I had to justify what I was doing for clearly he felt that my decision was very strange. So I explained. I had always been disappointed not to have made the trip to Pailin during the years when I had worked in the embassy. Located in Battambang province Pailin had an air of mystery attached to it for the foreign community in Phnom Penh. Very few foreigners visited the settlement, which was a gem mining centre with a Burmese, or more correctly Shan community, controlling the mining trade. There was another consideration, I went on. General de Gaulle's long-awaited visit to Cambodia was about to take place and everything in the capital was going to close down during the visit. I had seen de Gaulle in Paris and had no particular interest in seeing him again, so now seemed like a good time to go. 'Pailin', he finally said, *'c'est le far ouest cambodgien!'*

The observation was accurate in geographical terms. Pailin is one of the most westerly settlements in Cambodia, situated close to the Thai border. But clearly more was implied. Was I to imagine Pailin as some Cambodian approximation of Dodge City or Tombstone with Cambodian gunslingers ready to draw their Buntline Specials at the hint of an insult? Surely this could not be what he had meant in describing Pailin as the far west? Had he himself ever been there? As I had expected there was a negative response to that last question. Out of the way provincial towns did not figure high on the list of places to go for members of the Phnom Penh elite. But, of course, he had friends who had been there, and he had talked about Pailin quite recently with the head of the National Police in Battambang, who was a friend and whom I should certainly go and see. As for the far west image, he went on, he was indeed speaking figuratively but what a lot of foreigners and many of his own countrymen did not realise was that Battambang province generally had something of a frontier character to it and that Pailin certainly was a settlement with its own very special identity.

Some of this I knew. Battambang province's history was distinctively different from those central provinces of Cambodia closer to Phnom Penh. For the whole of the nineteenth century Battambang was under Thai control, though the administration that followed the directions of the court in Bangkok was, in fact, Cambodian. Both before and during this period of Thai control Battambang showed a disproportionate capacity to produce outstanding officials for the court in Phnom Penh. When working in the Phnom Penh archives I had been struck by this fact as I studied the personal dossiers of Cambodian officials at King Norodom's court in the second half of the nineteenth century. As for Pailin's particular identity, once again the archives had something to say about this. Only a few weeks before I had read through a report on Pailin prepared at some date shortly before the First World War. A Lieutenant Brunet had slowly made his way into Pailin on horseback to find a settlement that had an appearance he regarded as 'more civilised' than that encountered in other Cambodian villages. The influence of the French colonial government in Cambodia hardly touched Pailin and trade was mostly with Thailand. Most distinctively of all the gem trade that provided the basis for Pailin's existence was in the hands of Shans from Burma. They had come to Pailin at the time when Battambang province was still administered as part of Thailand and when an English company, Siam Syndicate Limited, had recruited Shans from British Burma to exploit the gem bearing soils about the settlement.

My friend bore with me. Like many Cambodians he had little interest in the details of past history. The present was what mattered and it seemed that all was not well in Battambang in general and in Pailin in particular. It was difficult to describe but the sense he had gained from his friends who had been in Battambang recently was that conditions in the apparently highly fertile countryside were such that there were murmurings of peasant discontent. And he had been told that in Pailin a small number of wealthy Burmese dominated the population along the lines of an American company town. Beyond that he did not have more details.

In 1971, the last time I visited Battambang, the only way to reach the provincial capital was by air. The Cambodian Communists quickly recognised the strategic value of cutting the highway and the rail link between Phnom Penh and Battambang once war broke out in 1970. In 1966 there was still a choice between the railway or a bus, with the former quite clearly the more attractive from the point of view of both comfort and reliability. Cambodian trains ran on time. This had little if anything to do with Sihanouk or his politics. Rather it was a reflection of that strong sense of *esprit de corps* that seems to be part of railway workers all over the world.

My fellow passengers seemed an unremarkable group, the same sort of mix as I had seen on the three other occasions when I had made this trip; Buddhist monks in their orange robes, ethnic Chinese merchants going back to their businesses in the provinces, matronly women who proved to have been in Phnom Penh buying the goods that they could not obtain in the settlements near the army camp where their husbands were posted, and a young man whose white shirt and pointed black shoes suggested he was a student taking advantage of the holidays accompanying General de Gaulle's visit to return to his home in the provinces. This last identification was right. He was a student in a private secondary school in Phnom Penh and while it was closed he was off to see his parents in Sisophon, a town lying northwest of Battambang city and only some thirty miles from the border with Thailand.

I was not surprised when he struck up a conversation. I was a foreigner and I was reading a book. The first fact was a matter of interest in itself since foreigners making this trip by train in 1966 were few and far between. And since I was reading a book I, like him, could probably be classed as an 'intellectual', a very elastic word in Cambodian student usage but one that they sincerely felt applied to them and set them apart from the mass of the people who did not go on to secondary school education. Where was I from? What was I doing in Cambodia? Why was I going to Battambang? This was a standard series of exchanges and I was only a little more surprised when the conversation shifted to broad political issues. My fellow passenger had clearly picked up the essentials of current Cambodian foreign policy as proclaimed by Sihanouk. The Thais and Vietnamese were Cambodia's traditional enemies. The United States had no reason to be in Vietnam. A united Communist Vietnam would not attack Cambodia because China had promised Prince Sihanouk that it would not allow this to happen.

For a while he was silent on the seat beside me and then he started speaking again, and this time I was not just surprised I was disconcerted. Was it possible that here was an *agent provocateur* sent to trap me into saying something critical of Sihanouk and his policies so that I could be expelled from the country? Then and now I was and am convinced that this was not the case. The heretical opinions that the young man offered me were a reflection of a feeling, far more widely held than I realised at the time, that Sihanouk's Cambodia provided no answer to the hopes and aspirations of the young men and women who had struggled, sometimes at the cost of real financial sacrifice, to work for a high school diploma or university degree. As he searched for the right French words to express himself the young man seemed to find the courage to review a whole range of topics from a point of view opposed to Sihanouk's policies and pronouncements. It was all very well for Prince Sihanouk to criticise young people for wanting to find jobs in the civil service, but what other jobs were there to fill? He and his friends could see little chance of employment of any kind that would take account of the education they had received. He knew of diploma holders who worked as coolies in the mines at Pailin and what could be more degrading than that for an intellectual? He had come to think that Sihanouk was not always right. Why was it necessary to be in a state of constant antagonism with Thailand? And how could Cambodians be sure that if the Communists won in Vietnam they would leave Cambodia alone as Sihanouk said would be the case? When Sihanouk was overthrown some three and a half years after I had listened to the young man there were some observers who found it hard to believe that many students in Phnom Penh greeted the event with joy. I did not.

The head of the National Police was ready to see me and to buy me an excellent dinner of venison. He was ready to go some way towards speaking frankly about the problems he faced in Battambang, but only in the most general terms. Yes, there were problems and there were certainly 'Communists' in the province. How many it was hard to say. He thought that there might be two thousand Communists in the whole of Cambodia, if what one was talking about was the men who were in the *maquis* (the scrub) and biding their time to strike. But that number did not take account of left-wing intellectuals who might or might not be ready to match action to their political opinions. One of the problems he saw was the presence of an increasing number of educated young people who could not find jobs that they considered good enough for them. The problem was not as aggravated in Battambang as it was in Phnom Penh, but it existed nonetheless. Then he made a comment to which I gave little importance at the time. As head of the National Police for the province he had to work with the army to try to prevent right-wing anti-Sihanouk insurgents, the Khmer Serei or Free Khmer, from slipping over the border to lay mines before returning to Thailand. His superiors saw this as one of the most important of his duties but he was convinced that the risk of real trouble lay in other parts of the province, closer to Battambang and from elements that were living permanently in Cambodia. This curious comment came at the end of our evening together. It seemed to fit with what my friend had said in Phnom Penh but it was clear that there was much more to be learnt.

I soon realised why so few foreigners travelled to Pailin. In a four-wheel drive vehicle the trip might have been bearable, but it is doubtful if even a Landrover could have made it comfortable. In an ancient bus the journey took more than four hours as we averaged some thirteen miles an hour to cover the fifty miles from the province capital to Pailin. The first twenty-five miles were only occasionally marred by potholes and corrugations, but once the road started winding into the hills the surface of the road deteriorated immediately. Frequently the surface disappeared altogether so that the bus picked its way between holes and over humps of what appeared to be not much more than a section of laterite that had been cleared of ground cover. When, at last, we reached Pailin I immediately thought of the far west image, for in a curious way it was right. Pailin town stretched along a single main unsurfaced street, its two-storeyed wooden houses with low verandahs did have a superficially striking resemblance to the archetypical town of a Western film.

Just how superficial the resemblance was became apparent the moment one raised one's eyes to look at the countryside surrounding the town. For there were the hills that almost surrounded Pailin, covered in the unrelieved dark green of tropical vegetation.

And on one of the nearer hills was the unexpected sight of a Buddhist pagoda built in the Burmese rather than the Cambodian architectural style. The Cambodian far west had little but isolation to share with the western frontier lands of nineteenth century America.

As I walked about the town and its outskirts I found the 'mines'. They were not at all what I expected. Many were only shallow trenches and holes in the ground with coolies lifting baskets of earth from the bottom to helpers at the top who then grubbed through the earth looking for stones. Larger enterprises were still far removed from a stereotyped image of a mine, consisting merely of trenches and holes but located close to running water that was used to sluice the earth away. It was hard to believe that this was a prime source for rubies and saphires. So too it had been hard to believe what the young man had told me the day before —that holders of high school diplomas dug in the ground for poor wages. I was soon to have confirmation. As I passed one of the holes I found myself addressed in excellent French. The young man who spoke to me had received five years of secondary education, though he was not in fact a diploma holder. There were others, he assured me however, who did have diplomas but who, like him, found the prospects for work elsewhere so limited that they had come to Pailin where the work was hard but there was always the chance that a rich find of stones could bring temporary relief from poverty and hard physical labour. He was clearly a person who resented his low position and who found the dominance of the Shans in Pailin—they owned the most productive mining sites *and* controlled access to the water necessary for washing away dirt from the gem stones—particularly galling. It would have been bad enough if he were working for a Cambodian in these conditions but to suffer them as a coolie for a foreigner, that was the final indignity.

Occasionally a cliché meets a writer's need. In the case of my brief experience in Battambang this was so. I really was, though I only partly understood it at the time, seeing the 'tip of the iceberg'. A bare six months after I visited Battambang city and travelled to and from Pailin, a rural insurgency erupted in the province which came to be hailed by the Communist leaders of Kampuchea as one of the great steps along their path to final victory in April 1975. Conditions in Pailin were bad at the time I visited that settlement. Later research by a French scholar, Raymond Blanadet, has shown that Pailin was experiencing major social and economic problems by 1966. Its population had grown sharply as the result of an influx of both ethnic Cambodian refugees who had fled from southern Vietnam and newcomers from other areas of Cambodia itself who sought the chance of sudden wealth so often thought to be available where mining enterprise takes place. The reality that existed was of long-established Shan mining entrepeneurs controlling both the best mining sites and the water. Although they owned only ten per cent of the land, the Shans controlled fifty per cent of the best gem yielding land. And they controlled access to water, demanding as much as twenty-five per cent of the value of any stones found when 'their' water was used in sluicing procedures.

More generally the population of that section of Battambang province through which I had travelled so slowly and uncomfortably on my way to Pailin was to prove the accuracy of the head of the National Police's gloomy forecast. As the result of an extraordinary range of factors including oppressive landlordism, usury, a poor rice crop, mismanagement of pioneer agricultural industries, and corrupt administration, the peasants of the southern region of Battambang province were brought to a point where they were ready to listen to those who advocated violent revolutionary solutions to their plight. The conditions in southern Battambang should not be taken to reflect the conditions that prevailed elsewhere in Cambodia in 1966. The far west did indeed possess a special character of its own and the disadvantages and deprivations suffered by its peasant farmers were of a different order to those experienced in regions less affected by landlordism.

When in response to conditions that had ceased to be tolerable and led by men who believed they had an ideology that would guide them successfully in their revolutionary struggle the peasants of Battambang became insurgents, they set the stage for a final drama that harked back to the far west catchphrase. A rebellion broke out in April 1967, centred initially around the village of Samlaut, and Sihanouk, egged on by his right-wing advisers who were now in a position of growing dominance, was furious. Just as he had always seen external criticism of Cambodia as representing criticism of his person so did he now come to see the internal rebellion in Battambang as a personal as much as a national challenge. Into his far west he sent not the United States cavalry but General Lon Nol's infantry. But the orders Lon Nol received had their antecedents in the punitive expeditions of the American cavalry against recalcitrant American Indians. What was important was suppression of the rebellion. How this was achieved was of little or no concern to Sihanouk. When I returned to Cambodia at the end of 1967 after an absence of just over a year Phnom Penh talk was full of what had happened. The suppression had been bloody. Resistance had been met with the greatest possible force. Lon Nol had been implacable and retribution had ranged from summary executions to the burning of villages. Ghoulish details were provided of trucks filled with severed heads that were sent from Battambang to Phnom Penh so that Lon Nol could be assured that his program was being followed. The '*far ouest cambodgien*' had more than lived up to my friend's description.

CHAPTER FIVE

The Passions of a Prince

It is hard to write about Prince Norodom Sihanouk in 1966 in a way that is always moderate, fair, and reasonable. For by that year much of his behaviour could not be classified in such terms. In the past journalists had too readily and glibly found a basis for mocking copy in some of Sihanouk's enthusiasms and more notable eccentricities. Sihanouk's decision to immerse himself in the business of film making as Cambodia lurched ever deeper into a morass of economic and political danger seemed calculated to ensure that he would once again be depicted as the 'playboy prince'. In another book I have argued that there was much more to Sihanouk's character and achievements than is suggested by such an epithet.* But the basis for that judgment depended on a review of Sihanouk's public and private life over a span of more than twenty years. If the focus narrows then one can see that what at times was a lack of balance in Sihanouk's judgment in earlier years had become, by 1966, something more, something dangerous both to his own position and to the survival of his state.

Since I am going to argue that Sihanouk's commitment to film making *was* a significant matter with serious political consequences and an important indication of his unwillingness, or incapacity, to face reality, I need to discuss, and in some cases dispose of, aspects of his life that too often have been seen as a cause for

---

*Politics and Power in Cambodia: The Sihanouk Years, 1973, Chapter 6.

indulgent foreign mirth. Sihanouk's relationships with women offered irresistible targets for a certain kind of Western newspaper and magazine. By the standards of the royal family in which he grew up his amorous adventures as a young man were unremarkable. By the mid-1960s his personal affairs had settled into a fairly stable pattern. A certain number of nights of each week were spent with Princess Suzanne, a cousin and the sister of Prince Norodom Kanthal. The other nights were spent with Monique, the beautiful part-Italian part-Cambodian woman for whom, beyond dispute, Sihanouk reserved his truest affection. Only these two women ever held the status of being Sihanouk's legal wives. There were occasional departures from this pattern and for a period in April 1966 *le tout-Phnom Penh* waited breathlessly to discover whether Sihanouk would succeed in bedding Prince Viriya's daughter, the niece of his wife, Suzanne. This was a matter on which the pedicab riders seemed particularly knowledgeable, and not just those who touted for custom outside the Hôtel le Royal and were members of the secret police. But, for the most part, none of this mattered politically, not in any event the sexual element. As Cambodian folk tales make clear the values of traditional society were robustly earthy and involved frank admiration for sexual capacity, both male and female. Kings were expected to be potent and most certainly not restricted to one consort. In seeking to report on Sihanouk's love life in titillating terms sections of the Western press were not only hypocritical—tacitly glossing over the sexual adventures of politicians in their own societies—they presented an inaccurate image in suggesting that Cambodians cared very much about whom it was Sihanouk took to his bed. Sections of the Cambodian elite did come to care, and to care very much, when Monique increasingly came to use her position as Sihanouk's consort to enrich herself, her family, and a staggeringly avaricious clique operating under her protection. This, however, was another issue.

A more serious criticism levelled against Sihanouk by foreigners and Cambodians alike related to how he treated his children. There were many of them, possibly in excess of thirty, though the very occasional official references to his offspring suggested the correct figure was half that number. But, for Cambodians, the numbers

were not important since kings—and neither Sihanouk nor his
subjects ever forgot that he had been the king for fourteen years
before his abdication in 1955—were expected to have many
children. What was important was that Sihanouk showed so little
interest in the education and welfare of the bulk of his rambling
brood. With a few exceptions he seemed to have little interest in
his children. His daughters he sought to have married off as
quickly as possible. As for his sons, he had on occasions publicly
despaired of them. He was simply not prepared, he finally insisted,
to take any responsibility for what happened if the daughters of
the Phnom Penh bourgeoisie took the risk of associating with his
sons. He had had his fill of tearful mothers with pregnant
daughters. Only in the case of his chosen successor, Norodom
Naradipo, and one or two others did Sihanouk display anything
like paternal concern.

Yet once again it would be wrong to view this situation as
having too much political significance. The Cambodians who
were concerned that Sihanouk did not exercise a stricter control
over his children were a minority of a minority, a small section
of the elite that worried in case the escapades of Sihanouk's
sons and daughters should undermine the stability of the state.
Once again the issue was not viewed in terms of personal
morality.

Perhaps a comment should be made, too, about Sihanouk's use
of horoscopes, mediums, and omens. Certainly, these played a part
in his life, but few if any observers can accurately say how large
a part. What did gossip in the Phnom Penh of 1966 have to say
on this subject? When it came down to essentials in fact
remarkably little. Following the advice of soothsayers Sihanouk
would, apparently, sleep in one royal residence rather than another
on occasion, so as to comply with omens or avoid malevolent forces.
He was known to regard the ashes of a favourite daughter, Kanthi
Bopha, who had died suddenly as a young child, as being in some
way a talisman so that he slept with a casket containing her ashes
beside his bed. He paid special honour to the memory of a distant
royal female ancestor whose body had, over a century before, been
recovered miraculously from the stomach of a great crocodile. The
spirit of Princess Nucheat Khatr Vorpheak could be reached
through a female medium and it was to her spirit that Sihanouk

is a beautiful femine inhabitant of paradise); 'The Enchanted Forest' (a fantasy in which Sihanouk appeared as the benevolent ruling spirit of the forest); 'Twilight over Angkor' (a film loosely linked to an attempted rebellion against Sihanouk in the Angkor region in 1959), and finally 'Joie de Vivre' (a rather more bitter examination of the personal lives of the Phnom Penh elite than that undertaken in 'Apsara'). Artistically none of the films had merit. I make my judgment on the basis of having seen 'Apsara' twice, after seeing long extracts from 'The Enchanted Forest' and after enduring most of 'Joie de Vivre'. I must admit that my comment on 'Twilight over Angkor' depends on second-hand information, which I accept. I have no reason to think that in this film alone the Prince in some manner moved beyond the banality of script and the amateurish character of his camera work that were so much a part of his other efforts. Possibly something of the seriousness with which the whole enterprise was treated may be gauged from an account of the first public showing of 'Apsara', an event I attended in May 1966. A description of that evening, and of the film, is revealing in other ways as well.

I was late in reaching the Ciné Lux. It had been raining and I had had difficulty in finding a *cyclopousse* (pedicab). Then once I had found one the security precautions that were in force for Sihanouk's attendance at the gala screening made it necessary to walk the last four hundred yards to the cinema. The result was an unexpected meeting with Sihanouk himself, for I had reached no further than the lobby when the Prince entered. While I stood ready to bow but hoping to look inconspicuous Sihanouk did not hesitate. I cannot imagine that he remembered me from the few times I had shaken his hand five and six years before. But with the graciousness that could truly be part of his character he approached and greeted me as if it were the most natural thing in the world for a somewhat shabbily suited (purchased in Hong Kong in 1960 and much worn in the interim) foreigner to be standing in the lobby as he passed through to his place of honour in the dress circle.

The evening was introduced by a master of ceremonies who

declaimed the reasons that lay behind Prince Sihanouk's having
decided to undertake the task of making Cambodia's first feature
film destined to be shown abroad to an international audience.
The Prince, we were told, had acted as 'scriptwriter, director and
producer' and in doing so he had conceived a 'fairyland' (*féerie*)
offered in the service of national solidarity.

A fairyland yes, yet more, for you have these scenes before your
eyes every day. But to place them in relief it is necessary, quite
deliberately, to eliminate precisely that everyday quality and to
choose scenes with the eye of the poet and the sensitivity of
the artist.
  Why has this full-length film been made?
  A saying has it that 'Frenchmen know nothing of geography',
but for a long time we have observed that this lack of knowledge
is not simply the preserve of the French. Let us deal solely with
the world of the cinema. For a film producer (even one of real
talent) what is Cambodia? The ruins of Angkor . . . *and that
is all*. So a run-of-the-mill script is hurriedly written, one or
two flashy stars are hired, one adds a mixture of eroticism and
violence, advance promotion dwells on the same old hackneyed
themes (stew made from snake's meat . . . scorpions lurking in
boots . . . the poverty of the people . . . a meagre existence that
must be defended against tigers, etc. . . . etc.) and the whole
lot is put in motion. That is the image of Cambodia current
in the four quarters of the globe.
  Is it any longer possible to ignore such ineptitudes, such
errors, whether voluntary or otherwise? Certainly not and the
Chief of State, more than any other, has felt this deeply. And
so, once again, faithful to his reputation as the 'Pioneer Prince'
he has taken up the challenge. So much the better for who is
more qualified than he to provide such a real picture of present
day Cambodia? . . .

Read in translation, away from Phnom Penh, this oration
probably appears even more extraordinary than it appeared at the
time. For, amazing though it may seem, such high-flown prose,
written by one or other of the Frenchmen in his employ, was not
notably unusual in Sihanouk's Cambodia, when it was Sihanouk

and his talents that were under review. What was more striking on this occasion was that before the audience was indeed able to glimpse Sihanouk's 'fairyland' it was first necessary to sit through a film made by the Chinese government of Sihanouk's visit to China the previous year. Lasting no less than an hour it was educational in the most essential sense. From the moment he arrived in China until he boarded his aircraft to leave Sihanouk was surrounded by people; thousands upon thousands, even hundreds upon hundreds of thousands of people. The effect was overwhelming and drew apprehensive giggles from the audience. How, the film seemed to be saying, can any Southeast Asian leader do other than pay attention to a country of such a size and with such an enormous population? What an honour, the message also seemed to be, for the leader of a country of a bare six million people to be received and accompanied in his travels by the leaders of a country such as China. Only occasionally did the point appear to be made in a more direct fashion. China's potential power seemed clearly summed up in the sequence that showed Prince Sihanouk reviewing a guard of honour, the short statured prince dwarfed by the towering soldiers, their faces grim and unmoving. Perhaps rather overlong, the film was professional in production and made its point.

Then came 'Apsara'. We, the audience, were seeing it in a less than fully edited form. Various versions were to be released in the future, it appeared. One, destined for the screens of the socialist world, would include a long speech by Nhiek Tioulong, playing the part of General Rithi, denouncing the 'imperialists'. The version for the non-socialist world would have this speech excised. For the moment, however, it was the basic story lasting more than two and a half hours we were seeing. General Rithi, a rich bachelor had decided to give up his long-term relationship with a voluptuous widow, played by a Royal Air Cambodge air hostess with the striking name of Saksi Sbong, in order to seek the hand of the beautiful Kantha Devi, star dancer of the royal ballet, played by Sihanouk's truly beautiful daughter Bopha Devi. But the ballet star's heart has already gone out to another, to a young pilot in Cambodia's air force, a part taken by one Prince Sisowath Chivanmonirak. The marriage between Rithi and Kantha Devi takes place but is never consummated. The young pilot is wounded while gallantly defending his country against an air attack from the Saigon regime and its American allies. General Rithi realises that he must not stand in the way of true love. The pilot and Kantha Devi are united. Rithi promises to marry his mistress. And the young pilot's brother, played by Sihanouk's son Norodom Narindrapong, provides the closing action of the film. Depicting a youth of perhaps thirteen years, he seeks to learn about life and love by throwing himself into the arms of a nurse in the hospital where his wounded older brother has been taken for treatment.

Despite all of the disclaimers made by Prince Sihanouk and his spokesmen 'Apsara' had absolutely nothing to do with the reality of Cambodia in 1966, unless it revealed that Sihanouk's vision of reality was far removed from that of the actual world. In a country where the sun shone constantly 'high personalities' drove here and there in one luxurious vehicle after another. I still have the script: Scene 1 (taken at Chamcar Mon, Sihanouk's personal palace) 'A Facel Vega driven by a pretty young woman'. Scene 6 (again at Chamcar Mon) 'General Rithi and Rattana get out of his Jaguar'. Scene 10 (on the Kirirom Plateau) 'Along a fine asphalted road, running through a magnificent pine forest, drives a black Cadillac convertible'. Scene 15 'An overview: arrival of the guests in glistening cars'. Scene 22 'The 230 S.L. stops at the foot of the monumental staircase leading towards the Mohanikay pagoda'.

From start to finish 'Apsara' was indeed a 'fairyland' depicting Sihanouk's fantastical vision of a country Cambodia never had been and never could be. Dirt, poverty, and disease were absent. The streets of the capital were free of the ubiquitous pedicabs that were so much a part of its normal life. 'Life' as it was led in Sihanouk's film revolved around receptions, parades, languorous moments in palaces and villas decorated in the worst of taste, and knockabout humour provided by Cambodia's best-known music hall comic who gloried in the nickname of 'Mandoline'. Only once, briefly, did the film capture anything that seemed in the least authentic, unless it was additionally the image of the more worthless of Cambodia's royal and wealthy citizens at thoughtless play. This was when the royal ballet, with Bopha Devi as its star, danced to the music of the traditional Cambodian orchestra. Yet even here Sihanouk chose to present the famous dancing troupe on the stage of the modern Conference Hall that had recently been constructed on the banks of the Tonle Sap River rather than in the usual setting of the Dance Pavilion within the Royal Palace.

The showing of 'Apsara' in May had been for a charity gala, and final points of continuity had not been settled. A print of the film was reprocessed in France to improve colour quality and with final editing under the Prince's guidance concluded, the way was now clear for a World Premier. The date chosen was just ten days before President de Gaulle was to arrive on his state visit. On 20 August Phnom Penh society was to have the opportunity to see the film in its completed form *and* rushes from the new film now under production, 'The Enchanted Forest'. Invitations had been sent abroad in the hope that special foreign delegations might be present at the premier, but to the best of my recollection none in fact came. The regrets of the Chinese Government were made public. No Chinese delegation would be present, the message came from Peking, 'because of the Cultural Revolution' that was in progress. I found no difficulty in purchasing a ticket for the premier.

On this occasion I arrived on time for an event that could not seem other than bizarre against the background of the preceding three weeks. This was the month that had seen Sihanouk driven to almost speechless rage by the attacks against the village of Thlok Trach. It was a time when negotiations of the greatest importance were going on between the Cambodian Government and the representatives of the Democratic Republic of Vietnam and the southern National Liberation Front concerning a border agreement. The economy was in continuing decline and Sihanouk was beginning to show public concern about the appeal to his country's youth of some left-wing politicians. Yet here was the same Prince Sihanouk about to preside over the premier of a film that not only lacked artistic distinction but was increasingly discussed in Phnom Penh elite circles in terms of the ridicule that it would bring upon the country. Could it be, people asked, that General Nhiek Tioulong was edging towards senility, agreeing to play the ageing lover as he did in the film and to utter lines of such banality? The question was one that I could understand even if I forbore to answer. For a feature of the film was the quite frequent use of French interspersed through the Khmer dialogue. Here from the script is the dialogue from the reconciliation scene between General Rithi (Nhiek Tioulong) and Rattana (Saksi Sbong):

> *Rithi:* . . . It is only in misfortune that one knows one's true friends. In you I have a true friend.
> *Rattana:* (ironically) Friend?
> *Rithi:* No! You will be my wife.
> *Rattana:* (overcome with joy) Oh my love. (Rithi takes her firmly in his arms. They fall on the bed.)
> *Rithi:* (gives her a passionate kiss while whispering) My dear one.

But even more important, it was increasingly being asked, how could Prince Sihanouk cope with the manifold difficulties that beset the country if he continued to devote so much of his time to this passion, for it was now clear that much more than a fad or hobby was involved?

I had never before heard such restrained applause accompanying Sihanouk's entry into a gathering as on that night and the applause at the conclusion of showing was brief, even perfunctory. Between the start and finish of the evening the audience was shown an edited version of 'Apsara' still running no less than two hours and twenty minutes. Apart from the improved quality of its colour the film appeared little changed from the version screened in May. Then there was the bonus of the excerpts from the new film in which Sihanouk and Monique both acted. The scene that stays most firmly fixed in my mind is of Sihanouk as the ruler of his enchanted forest waiting to receive Monique, a worldling who has suddenly and mysteriously been transported to his magical kingdom. Neither my memory nor my journal tells me what Monique was wearing. But for Sihanouk's garb there is no need for a written prompt. He was wearing a jacket of the sort associated with Pandit Nehru. In Sihanouk's case, however, it was tailored from some sort of 'luminous' cloth, perhaps of gold lamé. Sihanouk's was not an unhandsome face, but he had among his range of habitual facial expressions a particular self-conscious smile that can only be described as a simper. As he simpered in his luminous golden jacket I was irresistibly reminded of Liberace. Here was not Sihanouk but an oriental Liberace on the screen of the Ciné Lux.

Nearly three and a half years later, when I saw the last of Sihanouk's films there were barely five weeks remaining of his rule over Cambodia. I did not know this as I travelled out to the Cinéma d'Etat to see 'Joie de Vivre', which the Prince described as his 'first film of passion'. But like many others I was aware of the rumours in the city that Sihanouk might not return from France. Sihanouk had left Cambodia for medical treatment in France at the beginning of January 1970. It was now mid-February, and on 18 April Sihanouk was deposed from his position as Chief of State.

Phnom Penh was a city gripped by malaise. Away from the capital more and more areas of the country lying along the eastern borders with Vietnam were out of the control of the Cambodian Government and being used as major staging and supply areas by the Vietnamese Communists. Most observers agreed there were fifty thousand Vietnamese Communist troops in Cambodia at this time. The Phnom Penh Casino that Sihanouk had decided to open in 1969 in order to provide desperately needed funds for the armed forces had been closed at the end of January 1970 as the realisation dawned that it had become both a symbol and a cause of the decline of morale in the capital. Whether or not the gossip of frequent suicides following gambling losses was accurate, the fact that these stories made the rounds was important. Rich and poor had gambled incessantly. A rule insisting that only those wearing shoes were allowed to enter had supposedly kept the poor away; an enterprising Chinese businessman had set up a shoe rental stall near the casino's entrance. When I attended the last night of the casino's existence I scarcely believed what I saw. I had seen gambling elsewhere—two-up in Broken Hill, roulette in London, fan tan in Macau—but never had I seen anything like this. I had not intended to gamble, but even if I had wanted to I doubt whether I would have succeeded in making my way through the packed ranks of players and would-be players that surrounded the tables. They spilled bank notes over the tables in a frenzied last effort to beat the odds. For *le petit peuple*, the little people of Sihanouk's speeches, this must have been a case where their fortunes did, quite genuinely, change hands.

So Phnom Penh in February 1970 was a city in a sombre, uncertain mood. I was still surprised when the young man pedalling my *cyclopousse* started speaking to me as he did. The immediate question came to mind. Was he one of those *pedaleurs* who worked for the secret police? It hardly seemed likely in this case. I had hailed him far away from the usual tourist haunts and his comments seemed both too bitter and too deeply critical to be other than genuine. His French was good; why should it not be, he said. After all he had gone to secondary school in Prey Veng. His parents were relatively prosperous farmers but he had been determined not to stay stuck in the provinces. Once in Phnom Penh he, like thousands of others, had found no work available except for the physically demanding labour of the docks or the pedicabs. Where was I going? To see Prince Sihanouk's latest film? I would not find many there to view it. And did I know there was another film showing with it; the film of the young pederast prince who was studying ballet in Europe? What a disaster life was!

If he was a secret policeman his disguise, both mental and physical, was remarkably convincing. Whatever the case his prediction of the size of audience was accurate. I was one of a scattered gathering of perhaps two dozen; a few Cambodians and the rest, so far as I could tell, East European diplomats and experts based in Phnom Penh. I arrived in time to see most of 'The Other Little Prince', a technically excellent film made in Czechoslovakia that showed Prince Norodom Sihamoni in a series of ballet sequences. Whether his sexual persuasions were as the pedicab man had said I do not know. Certainly this was the received view in Phnom Penh. The Czech film was followed by a production of the Cambodian Ministry of Information, 'The Pioneer Prince'. This was a poorly made exercise in cinemato-graphic sycophancy. Fortunately it was short. Then, finally, came 'Joie de Vivre'.

'It was dreadful,' I noted in my journal. 'The technical standard was just as bad as 'Apsara', indeed four years seem to have brought little change in either technique or the quality of the story line.

This one recounted the faithlessness of a woman (the inimitable and full-bosomed former airlines hostess Saksi Sbong plays the part) and shows her hopping in and out of bed with various minor princes, General Nhiek Tioulong *et al.* The royal family is depicted as constantly absorbed with lust and gambling—perhaps this is not so far wrong—and shows them living in villas furnished at great expense and in the worst taste, driving everywhere in Cadillacs. After two hours I could bear no more and left.'

Not without difficulty as it happened. As I tried to leave in a manner that would draw little attention to me I succeeded in doing exactly the opposite. The exits along the side walls of the cinema hall, through which I tried to slip away quietly, were all locked and it was necessary to leave by the main door at the back of the hall, an exit that opened and closed with a loud squeaking of hinges and clanging of the horizontal rods against which it was necessary to push in order to release the floor catches. The *cyclopousse* that had brought me to the Cinéma d'Etat was not waiting for my return fare, an apparent confirmation that the rider was what he claimed to be; another discontented youth of some education adrift in the capital.

Cambodia did not become a radical Communist state because Prince Sihanouk devoted many hours to making films of poor artistic quality instead of spending that time in reviewing matters of state. Quite obviously a myriad other factors were involved. But if one is searching for an explanation of the decision of those on the Cambodian right to mount their coup against Sihanouk in March 1970, then the issue of his film making does have real importance. Sihanouk's films were a highly visible symbol of what so many of his critics deplored. In the past he had insisted on determining policy and was prepared to see that policy once determined was implemented. From the middle 1960s onwards he showed an ever growing readiness to opt out of any involvement in state matters that required going beyond the enunciation of policies. And, in the view of his critics, it became even harder to have him lay down policy. Some would argue that the time he spent making his films did not represent even a significant cause for the decline of Sihanouk's state. Multiple factors, both external and internal, were undoubtedly involved and different observers will give them different weight. As I observed Cambodia in 1966 and each subsequent year until Sihanouk's overthrow I had no doubt that for those men who had their hands on the levers of power, both in Phnom Penh and in the provinces, the films Sihanouk made and the time he spent making them were a highly important and annoying symbol of the character of the Prince's rule. I have also come to believe that the films, along with so much else in Sihanouk's Cambodia, could only have given deep offence to men on the left.

CHAPTER SIX

Portraits 1. The Soldier

When I first met him in 1960 he had just been promoted, at the age of thirty, captain in the Cambodian army. The son of a judge he was by any standard a member of the elite. Yet by the standards of that elite, Kim Kosal was a man apart. He had never, I was told, been much interested in the routine of bars and girls that was followed by most of his contemporaries. It was not that his sexual interests lay elsewhere, a mutual friend hastened to tell me. The plain fact was that the captain was 'serious'. Sufficiently serious, indeed, to decide in 1959 that it was important for a Cambodian army officer to speak English as well as French and so to take himself off to England, at his own expense, to master the language. He had also been sufficiently skilful and dedicated to be selected to represent Cambodia in the equestrian events of the 1956 Olympic Games. By 1966 Kim Kosal was a *commandant*, a 'major' in direct translation, but as the Cambodian army followed French practice this rank usually involved command of a battalion rather than a company which would be a major's normal responsibility under British practice. As a battalion commander he held a key position with his headquarters at Kompong Chrey in Takeo province, a little more than fifty miles south of Phnom Penh and about fifteen miles west of the border with Vietnam.

Where Takeo province borders Vietnam the topographic conditions have always presented endless opportunities for guerilla forces and countless difficulties for conventional forces seeking to contain and eliminate them. The flat ground of the region was

59

criss-crossed by watercourses, some natural, some man-made. Who could tell which of the countless sampans that glided along the creeks and canals carried men with weapons rather than farmers and fishermen? During the wet season vast areas were submerged beneath floodwaters and the always poorly demarcated border between Cambodia and Vietnam became even more difficult to define. But not all the land was flat. Not far from Kompong Chrey rise the low mountains of the Kirivong, the 'Ring of Mountains'. A little further distant to the southeast lie the fabled Seven Mountains. Fabled, famous, some would say the infamous Seven Mountains. The seven features so frequently spoken of collectively are scarcely impressive in statistical terms. The highest rises only a bare two thousand feet above sea level and the peaks rise haphazardly over an area of perhaps two hundred square miles. It is their setting that lends them scale for they suddenly jut upwards from a dead flat plain and this contrast between the unrelieved flatness of the Mekong delta and the abruptly rising Seven Mountains gives them a physical significance that would be lacking if they were located in a different and less flat landscape. The mountains were always striking to see but never more, for me, than when I saw them while flying over the delta in a light aircraft. The vast rice fields of southern Vietnam stretched towards the easternmost region of Cambodia. It was July and there seemed to be as much water as land beneath us. Rain squalls added to the water already lying below, but thirty miles away on the western horizon there was a break in the clouds so that the sun shone down on the Seven Mountains, giving even greater emphasis to the contrast between their height and what lay around them.

This contrast had long been seen as giving the Seven Mountains a special character. Both Vietnamese and Cambodians saw them as magical sites, places for hermits to live, for pagodas and shrines to be built. The mountains with their thick forest cover were also locations to which bandits withdrew, to defy the efforts of governments, whether colonial or otherwise, to track them down. During both the First and Second Indochinese Wars the Seven Mountains were used as retreats by the Vietnamese Communists. Not only Communists, but other forces were located near and on the slopes of the Seven Mountains. Some of these were the Khmer Serei, the Free Khmers, whose leader, Son Ngoc Thanh, was

Sihanouk's oldest and most bitter opponent. The reasons for Son Ngoc Thanh's hatred of Sihanouk had roots that stretched back to the 1940s. In 1966 he and his followers were a minor but not insignificant element in the combined efforts of the Americans and the Saigon regime to prevent a Communist victory in southern Vietnam.

Not all the details are clear even now but the essential features of the part played by the Khmer Serei have long been known. At best Sihanouk and his policies were distrusted by the American military and by the American intelligence community concerned with Vietnam. In these circumstances the CIA gave support to Son Ngoc Thanh and the troops he had gathered about him. These troops were almost all ethnic Cambodians born into the substantial ethnic Cambodian minority located in southern Vietnam. For convenience Son Ngoc Thanh is usually described as 'right-wing', though what this description really meant by 1966 is hard to say. The thought that dominated his life was to bring Sihanouk down. From the point of view of the Americans and the Saigon authorities Son Ngoc Thanh was a useful 'plus'. If Sihanouk ever should be toppled from his place as Cambodia's Chief of State then perhaps Son Ngoc Thanh could again show the capacity for political leadership that he had undoubtedly demonstrated in the 1940s and early 1950s. More immediately, his forces could be used to try to hunt down Communist forces believed to be lurking in parts of the Seven Mountains which straddle the border of Cambodia and Vietnam.

How successful the Khmer Serei were in locating and killing Communists is unclear. What was quite certain in 1966 was that Khmer Serei forces were slipping into southern Takeo province to carry out sabotage missions that were quite unrelated to the war being fought in Vietnam. They carried out occasional ambushes, but more usually they left behind mines and plastic explosives that took their toll in civilian lives, wrecked bridges, and cratered roads.

It was this problem, among many others, that was now the responsibility of the major whom I knew. I had met him again in Phnom Penh by chance, for the centre of the city was not large and chance meetings repeatedly occurred in the small number of shops and cafés that the Cambodian elite frequented. Now Kim Kosal was married, to the half-sister of the princely friend whose amazement at my intention to visit Pailin I have already described. Having met and reminisced about mutual friends, to my delighted surprise he invited me to spend a weekend with him at the house he had at the Kompong Chrey military base. So early on a Thursday morning in the middle of June I boarded a bus and set off for Kompong Chrey.

The road to Kompong Chrey passes through the capital of Takeo province and then continues south through regions of Cambodia that in 1966 still had a high proportion of Vietnamese settlers. Kompong Chrey itself, apart from the presence of the large army camp, had little to distinguish it from dozens of other settlements of a similar size throughout Cambodia. There were perhaps fifty Chinese shophouses lining the main street, and a population of about a thousand. This population was overwhelmingly Chinese for in rural areas such as this the Cambodians continued to live, with only limited exceptions, in their scattered villages. The army camp was just to the east of the township and it was not hard to sense some of the problems of being a Cambodian army officer in 1966. The camp area was tidy but strangely silent. One reason for this lay in the number of vehicles that were so obviously out of commission. As Kim Kosal later explained to me he felt himself lucky if half of the vehicles allotted to him were working. The jeeps and trucks that were available for his troops were old and had been poorly maintained. Since Prince Sihanouk had severed relations with the United States the army had become desperately short of spare parts for its transport vehicles. Even if he had half of the vehicles in service he was frequently so short of fuel that they could only be used sparingly. And, he went on ruefully, I should not be surprised if his men were not turned out with the smartness that might be expected in a military unit. For months he had been promised a shipment of new uniforms that was urgently needed but it still had not arrived.

For the next two days, particularly in the evenings, we talked a great deal. I learnt that he had been a soldier for fifteen years, including a period in the First Indochina War when he had fought, as a non-Communist, against the French. Now with this his first important command he had units from his battalion spread all over the province. There was always the possibility of some incursion by Saigon forces, but what kept him and his men busy were the infiltrators and saboteurs. Only two weeks before he had had to defuse two mines placed under one of the bridges on the road out of Kompong Chrey to the south. It was not an experience upon which he cared to dwell.

The verandah of his house looked to the east across dead flat ground. As we sat talking in the evening we could see the illumination flares being put up over their garrisons by the Saigon forces who were in some cases little more than fifteen miles away. From time to time there would be the distinctive rumble of artillery barrages. It was a curious background for a conversation that ranged over many subjects on an otherwise still night. Kim Kosal did not believe that anyone other than Sihanouk could have succeeded in achieving as much as had been achieved in the period up to the early 1960s. It was Sihanouk who had found a way to twist France's arm and so to gain independence in 1953. It was Sihanouk who, after his abdication in 1955, succeeded in finding a political formula that submerged the endlessly squabbling political factions within an all-embracing national movement, the Sangkum Reastr Niyum (People's Socialist Community). Sihanouk had succeeded in keeping Cambodia largely at peace. But something seemed to have gone very wrong.

He had heard, he went on wryly, that the Prince had dedicated his new film 'Apsara' to the officers and men of the Cambodian armed forces. He was sure that Sihanouk was sincere in doing this, but he wondered whether the Prince was aware of how short the army was of men, of equipment, of money, indeed of everything. If any improvements were to be made in the camp at Kompong Chrey then he had to find the money for this himself. If a roof in the camp needed replacement or repair he could expect no assistance from Phnom Penh. It was up to him to find the money and the materials. He was not entirely dependent on his officer's salary but many of his brother officers were not as fortunate as he. In these circumstances was it surprising that many officers supplemented their inadequate salaries through corruption?

Corruption, indeed, was a subject to which he returned time

and again in our extended conversations. Corruption, he made clear, was pervasive, and of course in these border areas it was particularly linked to rice smuggling. But not only to rice smuggling. The shops of Kompong Chrey were stocked with a wide variety of tinned goods smuggled in from Vietnam. There was little he could do about this, even if he felt a need to do so. For by comparison with the traffic in rice the illegal importing of these consumer items was a petty thing. What it illustrated, however, was the manner in which everyone was being touched by the disease of corruption. Did I think that he could survive if he did not at very least accept what was going on? What was most disturbing to him about the problem of corruption in Cambodia was that it spread from the very top, from circles close to the Prince and the Prince's government. It was only to be expected that Chinese merchants in Kompong Chrey would seek to benefit from the opportunities that were presented to them. He regretted that so many of his army colleagues were deeply involved in corrupt practices, and he did not claim to be totally outside the system himself. But what made the situation so dangerous was the acceptance and the encouragement of corrupt practices on a vast scale by those who should be the first to see what dangers lay in the path of a country that risked becoming consumed by corruption.

More than anything else, I was struck by his capacity for detachment as he reviewed the problems of his country and the part he had to play. He seemed saddened rather than bitter. He had a remarkably detached view of the war that was going on so short a distance across the border that his troops guarded. He believed the United States commitment in Vietnam was mistaken, that it would not in the long run succeed in halting the advance of the Vietnamese Communists. The prospect of a united Communist Vietnam concerned him, of course, so that like most if not all of his fellow officers he was not greatly troubled by the fact of Vietnamese killing Vietnamese. But the American involvement carried with it risks to Cambodia, above all the risk that the war might spill over Vietnam's borders in a way that had not yet happened. As for the Khmer Serei, he could even understand their actions, though this would not affect his dedication to hunting them down and if necessary killing them. Membership of the Khmer

Serei, he judged, gave these Cambodians whose homes were in southern Vietnam an opportunity to belong to something. If they had remained as peasants in their villages they would have been a prey to both sides in the conflict. He doubted that many of them fought for the defence of a particular political belief or idea. Such might be the case for their leaders but not for the rank and file. Indeed, he asked in another of those questions that I had learned not to try to answer, how many soldiers in any army fight for a political belief?

On the trip back to Phnom Penh and for days afterwards the question nagged in my mind: 'Could Kim Kosal be regarded as in any sense representative of the Cambodian officer corps?' In terms of his thoughtfulness and probity the answer surely had to be 'no'. But in terms of the problems he was dealing with—the lack of money, the broken-down vehicles, the absence of spare parts, of fuel, and even of uniforms—it seemed almost certain that his experience had parallels throughout Cambodia. Later observation seemed to confirm that this was so. And the situation that existed in 1966 deteriorated even further as the closing years of Sihanouk's rule over Cambodia ran their course. The army, or more particularly its officer corps, was a conservative body. The officers who had experienced the days of fat while American military aid was given to Cambodia increasingly resented the lean years from the middle 1960s. In allowing discontent to develop within his armed forces Sihanouk made one of his most serious political errors. He was later to say that he had misjudged the fidelity of General Lon Nol. He had never conceived that Lon Nol, in his role both of army commander and politician, would turn against him. But Lon Nol did and it is clear that in doing so he acted with the support of a disillusioned officer corps embittered and frustrated by their experience in the latter 1960s.

I saw Kim Kosal once more in 1966, but never again after that. He was still alive in 1971 and was, as I would have expected, in a combat area. Mutual friends told me that he believed he had no choice but to continue to serve in an army to which he had devoted his life. Much later I learnt that as the Cambodian Communist net drew tighter about Phnom Penh in late 1974 and early 1975 Kim Kosal, now a colonel, was prevailed upon to join the Lon Nol government as Minister for Communications. Relatives living outside the country urged him to leave while it was still possible. An honest man, he felt he had a duty to perform, and he believed the United States would not abandon its allies. He remained and the relatives who had urged him to leave believe he died very shortly after Phnom Penh was occupied by the Cambodian Communists.

CHAPTER SEVEN

Portraits 2. The Priest

It did not take me very long to find that my interest in the details of Cambodian history in the second half of the nineteenth century was not widely shared in Phnom Penh. History, in the quasi-scientific Western sense, was simply not part of Cambodian cultural patterns. The great French orientalist, George Coedès, had written about this attitude nearly fifty years before, and he had reiterated his view when I spoke with him in Paris before I returned to Phnom Penh in 1966. This does not mean that Cambodians were uninterested in history, but for most Cambodians, even the best educated, precise chronology and the weighing of causal factors had little to do with how to view the past. At first, therefore, I felt disappointed. I had access to members of some of the great families that had been important in the nineteenth century, both to sections of the royal family and to descendants of the semi-hereditary officials who were still important in contemporary Cambodia. Initially, however, talking to them about 'History' had been an unproductive business. Then someone suggested I consult Father Tep Im, a Cambodian Catholic priest.

Little has ever been written about the Cambodian Catholic community. Its size when compared with the predominant Buddhist community was infinitesimal. In 1966 there were perhaps three thousand *Cambodian* Catholics in the country in a total population of between six and seven million. There were other adherents to Catholicism, of course. Many in the remaining French community were Catholics, whether devoutly or nominally, but the total number of French citizens probably did not exceed two or three thousand. The other sizeable Catholic community was that found among the Vietnamese minority. Just how large this group was I never clearly established. Certainly it was much larger than the Cambodian Catholic community and there were many foreigners who were unaware that a group of Cambodians which belonged to the Roman Church even existed.

The nucleus of the Cambodian Catholic community was formed by the descendants of Iberians who had settled in Cambodia over the previous two or even three hundred years. These men had taken local wives but they and their descendants had retained their religion and their names. The Phnom Penh telephone directory listed such names as Fernandez, Diaz, de Lopez, and de Monteiro, and members of these families filled roles, in larger numbers than might have been expected given their size in relation to the overall community, in the public service, in the military, and in politics. The other significant and definable group in this community was made up of Khmer Krom (Cambodians from 'Lower Cambodia', those areas of modern southern Vietnam that were once under Cambodian rule and retained substantial ethnic Cambodian minorities). While France had colonial control over the whole of Indochina there was a significant inflow of Khmer Krom into Cambodia. Many rose to high positions in the Cambodian administration that continued to function alongside the French colonial government, or 'protectorate' as it was termed. Among these Khmer Krom were some who had been converted to Christianity at one or other of the mission establishments that the Roman Catholic Church maintained in southern Vietnam.

Then there was the smallest group of all, the Cambodians who were neither descended from Iberian stock nor from the Khmer Krom ethnic minority. Their numbers were few, but once again they tended to come from the middle or upper ranks of Cambodian society. Father Tep Im himself was the son of a teacher and his grandfather had been a court official. In 1966 he could point to various relatives in positions of some prominence in the administration. In his case his father had not been a Catholic but his mother had been and there had been no opposition to his being brought up in the faith. He judged that those other Cambodians who belonged to the Catholic Church and who did not fall into the category of being of Iberian descent or Khmer Krom were most likely to have come to their religion as he did; through the insistence of a mother who was already a practicing Catholic.

As a priest Father Tep Im was, in 1966, one of four Cambodians who had been ordained. He was a man of notable intellectual achievements, with a doctorate from the Gregorian University in Rome. His academic specialisations had been in theology, canon law, and history. In connection with the last he had written a thesis on the activities of the first Catholic missionaries who worked in Cambodia in the sixteenth and seventeenth centuries. I had found someone with whom I could discuss historical problems. And I had found a man who as priest and scholar had a remarkable understanding of Cambodian society.

Talking with Father Tep Im the first time I met him, in 1966, made me sharply conscious of the need to think further about an aspect of Phnom Penh 'life' that had been puzzling me. When I had first come to Cambodia in 1959 it had not been surprising that there should have been so many Frenchmen in the capital. It had only been six years since independence and France in Cambodia as elsewhere in its former colonial possessions set great store by maintaining close links at every possible level. What seemed strange twelve years after independence was that Prince Sihanouk still placed such heavy reliance on Frenchmen in his personal secretariat. They wrote his speeches, ran his magazines and the semi-official national newspaper, and provided economic guidance. This was something to think about and the need to do so was emphasised by the comments Father Tep Im made concerning the vital necessity for the Cambodian Catholic Church to rid itself of residual links with France. He noted, for instance, that the Catholic cathedral in Phnom Penh was considered to be within the jurisdiction of the French Roman Catholic Church. Since this was so it had as its Bishop a Frenchman. French priests still continued to be active in Cambodia, but only very occasionally did any of them speak Cambodian. In this they made a curious contrast with their fellow French priests in Vietnam who almost always possessed some capacity in Vietnamese. Only since Vatican II had the mass been celebrated in Cambodian, and only very recently had the Bishop agreed to permit the occasional Cambodian mass to be said in the Cathedral.

What was involved for Father Tep Im was the need to make

a clear break with the colonial period and the relationships that
had accompanied it. He and his fellow Cambodian priests had
to think about the Cambodian Catholic Church in Cambodia, in
Cambodian terms. They had to change the way their non-Catholic
fellow countrymen viewed Catholicism, a view that was summed
up in the faith being described as *sassena barang*, the 'religion
of the European foreigner'. In 1966 Father Tep Im looked ahead
to an uncertain future. He did not think it impossible for changes
to take place that would lead to Cambodia becoming some form
of socialist state, perhaps with some similarities to Yugoslavia. In
such an event he believed the Cambodian Catholic Church could
survive, provided it was truly Cambodian.

As I came to know Father Tep Im better, meeting from time
to time over several months, so did I increasingly come to value
his perception and understanding of both historical and contemporary Cambodian affairs. He had been at school with Sihanouk
in Saigon and saw the Prince as a man of lively intelligence, but
of easily swayed character. His character made him a prime target
for the flattery of those who wished to advance their position or
their policy. This priest was not simply knowledgeable concerning
his own religion but offered many insights into contemporary
Cambodian Buddhism. What he had to say gave further weight
to the impression that I was gaining of a consistent pattern of
'politics' beginning to matter in Cambodia in a fashion that had
not existed five or six years before. As Father Tep Im saw the
situation, a section of the Buddhist Church in Cambodia was being
drawn into playing a political role that was distinctively new.

Except within the narrowest definition of politics or political
life the Buddhist Church in Cambodia always has had political
overtones associated with it. In the nineteenth century during the
period of Vietnamese occupation the Buddhist monks played a vital
role in maintaining the concept of a Cambodian national identity.
In a rather obscure but nonetheless certain fashion the Buddhist
monks, and particularly those from the major monasteries in
Phnom Penh, sought to resist French efforts to undermine or
change basic features of Cambodian life such as the writing system
for recording the Cambodian language. In the late 1930s and early
1940s the slow growth of a Cambodian nationalist movement had
clear links with the Buddhist Institute in Phnom Penh. But what

was significant about this form of Buddhist political activity was its essentially national character. It was not concerned with advancing the interests of a single party or individual. Matters had now changed and in 1966 one of the two sects that made up the Buddhist Church in Cambodia was being used politically. Whether this was being done at Sihanouk's direction or as the result of a decision taken by some member of his inner circle was unclear. In seemed impossible to believe that the Prince was unaware of what was happening.

Cambodians follow the Theravada form of Buddhism, the Southern or 'Lesser Vehicle' form that draws its roots from Ceylon (Sri Lanka). By far the largest number of Cambodians are adherents to the Mohanikay sect of Theravada Buddhism. But a smaller number are members of the Thommayut sect, a reformed and somewhat aristocratic sect that had been founded in Thailand by King Mongkut in the mid-nineteenth century and then introduced into Cambodia by members of the Cambodian royal family who had lived for long periods in the Thai court at Bangkok. Monks from the Thommayut sect had rigourously refused to engage in anything that might be described as political activity. But the same was not true of the monks of the Mohanikay sect. Recently, Father Tep Im told me, monks of this order had taken to using the occasion of their sermons to the faithful to devote much praise to Prince Sihanouk, to his policies both domestic and foreign, and to the general clairvoyance of his thought. Father Tep Im believed that this dabbling in political affairs was deeply resented by the more conservative elements of Cambodian opinion in Phnom Penh. He was less sure as to the reaction of the peasant farmers living in the countryside. They might not see the monks' activities as improper behaviour. He felt sure, however, that many among the Phnom Penh elite did.

How did this urbane, highly educated and highly devout man see the future as he looked forward from 1966? He saw it in terms of revolution, a revolution that was already in the making but one that probably would not occur until Sihanouk's death. The Cambodian Catholic community was small and concentrated in Phnom Penh and Battambang, but it had links with many other regions of the country. As Father Tep Im and his fellow priests pursued their pastoral duties all over the country they felt that discontent was much greater than many observers, including Cambodians, realised. He was struck, in particular, by the discontent present in Battambang province. What he was describing was not something that could be easily defined or quantified. One thing he did not doubt; change was on the way and he and his fellow Cambodian priests would have no easy path to follow.

More than four and a half years passed before I saw this priest again. Revolution, or more accurately a coup d'état, had come more quickly than he had expected so that by early 1971 Cambodia was a country rent by war and Sihanouk was a pensioner in Peking. Finding Father Tep Im again had proved difficult. There had been no one at the Hoalong church, the place where we had always met before, when I went looking for him. So I turned to the presbytery beside the Phnom Penh cathedral. When I asked for the whereabouts of Father Tep Im I was told that he was no longer in Phnom Penh. I would find him in Battambang. To visit Battambang now that Cambodia was at war was a very different business from the easy train or bus travel of other days. But I wanted to see this interesting man again and the antiquated Dakotas that made the flight between Phnom Penh and Battambang were supposed to be reliable.

Once in Battambang I dredged from my memory the location of another presbytery, one that in years gone by had been used by French missionary priests. It still was and I again asked for assistance in finding Father Tep Im. I was given the necessary directions and nothing more. Not until I reached the *Eveché*, the bishop's residence, and saw the episcopal ring upon his hand did I learn that the priest I had known in 1966 was now Bishop Tep Im, Apostolic Prefect of Battambang. The failure of either of the French priests to tell me that Father Tep Im was now a bishop was a confirmation of all that he had said in 1966 of the readiness of his French colleagues to treat Cambodian priests as junior partners.

At first glance Bishop Tep Im seemed unchanged from the man I had known in 1966. He still had the same strong but welcoming face, the same athletic appearance. But there was some change, even if it was not easily definable. I was not, I was sure, seeing change engendered as the result of apostolic succession. He and I had always joked about my being a lapsed Australian Protestant who had come to have a friendly acquaintanceship with a Cambodian Catholic priest. It seemed one of the more unlikely conjunctions of interests and identities, but we each respected the other's faith or lack of it. The suggestion of change in his face was surely related to more immediate earthly concerns. He was a man who had seen what war meant and was going to mean to Cambodia. He had seen the bodies of Vietnamese massacred by the Phnom Penh government's forces in an atavistic bloodletting that had no better cause than the desire to make ancient enemies suffer. He had already seen the results in Battambang of the atrocities that both sides in the war now being fought in Cambodia appeared to regard as the norm for military behaviour. Looking back I suspect he had a fairly clear-eyed view of what the ultimate end of that war might be and that his 1966 hopes for a Yugoslavian style of socialism had now been significantly amended.

But we talked little of the war and much more of history and his own current and long-term project to translate the Bible into Cambodian. A translation existed, prepared by evangelical missionaries from the United States, but he did not regard it as satisfactory. It was excessively literal and could not be read with ease even by a highly educated Cambodian. Might it be possible for me to send him a copy of the New English Bible for he was sure that this would be of the greatest assistance to him in his translation efforts?

I did not see Bishop Tep Im when I returned to Cambodia a second time in 1971 but I left a copy of the New English Bible to be forwarded to him. The last communication I had from him thanked me for it and spoke of how he tried at the end of each day to translate some passages, however short, using a Latin, French, and English Bible to guide him towards the preparation of a Cambodian version. He was still in Battambang when the new Communist regime took power in April 1975. Several reports agree that he was executed before the end of that month.

CHAPTER EIGHT

Portraits 3. The Revolutionary

One night in early May of 1966 I shared an excellent dinner of Vietnamese food with a Cambodian acquaintance. Over our meal he told me that he had become a Communist. At the time I did not realise that this was what he was telling me. And he was never so direct as to say bluntly what I have just recorded. But that Poc Deuskomar had become a Communist, and that this was what he was telling me in an indirect fashion, became quite clear when he fled from Phnom Penh in July 1968, to emerge some time later as a second level leader among the forces fighting the Phnom Penh regime of Marshal Lon Nol. In 1966, while we ate *pho* soup and seasoned shrimp paste cooked on sugar cane, I was aware that my acquaintance had undergone a profound political and personal transformation over the years since I had first met him. What I did not recognise then, however, was just how great that transformation had been and how bitterly he had come to view the society within which he lived.

To gain some understanding of Poc Deuskomar it is necessary to know something of the Poc family. For hundreds of years members of this family had been among the most talented and the least trusted of the great semi-hereditary official families linked to the Cambodian court. The family had strong connections with Battambang province in western Cambodia and in the late eighteenth century a member of the family had played a prominent part in the events that led to Battambang passing under Siamese suzerainty. The Poc role in this affair was never forgotten or forgiven by sections of the Cambodian royal family. Later, at the

74

very end of the nineteenth century, another Poc was pushed to high office by the French over the bitter objections of King Norodom I who believed him to be untrustworthy and ready to compromise the ruler's interests in favour of those of the colonial power. In the period after the Second World War there was yet another case of a Poc siding with forces opposed to Cambodian royalty. Poc Khun was an ally of the Khmer Issarak leader, Son Ngoc Thanh, in Sihanouk's eyes the ultimate form of betrayal by one of his countrymen.

Against this record had to be placed the undoubted talents displayed by successive generations of the family. When I first met Poc Deuskomar in 1959 one of his uncles was a senior Cambodian diplomat who was about to take up his appointment as the first Cambodian Ambassador to Australia. Another uncle held a high judicial post in Phnom Penh. Then there was his aunt, a formidable lady who was married to no less a person than Prince Sisowath Monireth, Sihanouk's uncle, the eldest surviving son of King Monivong who had died in 1941, and the man who many had thought would be his father's successor. The Pocs might be distrusted but their talents were valued and they had links with powerful friends.

Poc Deuskomar, himself a member of the foreign service, was one of the first Cambodians I came to know on the basis of more than a passing acquaintance. His features showed the readiness of past members of his family to marry European women, and his own wife was French. At some stage, whether in France where he had been educated or elsewhere, he had encountered racial prejudice in a fashion that he could not dismiss or forget and as he planned to travel to Australia in advance of his uncle he was concerned as to how Australians would receive him. Events were to prove that he and his uncle had more to fear from their own countrymen, once they were established in Canberra, than they did from mine.

It was not until 1966 and my first extended conversation of that year with Poc Deuskomar that I learnt the full story. In 1960 the well-known Australian journalist, Denis Warner, had visited Phnom Penh. In Western eyes there was nothing untoward in his report but the copy that he filed following this visit was regarded by the always sensitive Cambodians as being derogatory to the royal family, and most particularly to Sihanouk's mother, Queen Kossamak. The predictable result was that Denis Warner was barred from re-entering Cambodia. A much less predictable result involved the sudden and unexpected return to Phnom Penh of both the Cambodian ambassador to Australia, Poc Thieun, and his nephew, Poc Deuskomar. Quite by chance, I witnessed this unexpected return. The duties of a Third Secretary in a small embassy are many and varied and on the day in question they involved my waiting at Phnom Penh's airport to collect a diplomatic bag. If Poc Thieun's return to Phnom Penh had been a normal matter the Australian embassy would have known of it. But the embassy did not and I suddenly and unexpectedly found myself among a small group of Poc relatives greeting a clearly distressed, even anguished Cambodian Ambassador to Australia and his nephew. Some few weeks later, with the suddenness of their return glossed over, the Poc uncle and nephew returned to Canberra.

Six years after the event Poc Deuskomar still felt bitter about what had happened. When Denis Warner's article appeared in the Australian press his uncle had entered a routine protest and left the matter there. It was Poc Thieun's failure to make what was regarded as a sufficiently strong protest, Poc Deuskomar recounted, that had led to his sudden and humiliating recall to Phnom Penh where he had to endure a protracted tongue lashing from Sihanouk; the threat of dismissal and disgrace, and the familiar complaint that the Poc family could never be trusted. Poc Thieun's own record and his powerful connections saved him from losing his ambassadorial appointment and preserved Poc Deuskomar's position as his uncle's protégé, but they had both seen how vulnerable they were. Their vulnerability was accentuated by the procedures the Cambodian Foreign Ministry followed to check on the political reliability of its officers. The Cambodian embassy in London, Poc Deuskomar explained, had as one of its tasks the duty of monitoring copies of Australian newspapers to see whether any slighting references to Cambodia or its leader appeared *and* to see whether such references drew prompt and sufficiently strong ripostes from the Cambodian embassy in Canberra. To this was added the presence in the Canberra embassy of an informer somewhere among the subordinate staff, who watched over the behaviour of his fellow Cambodians.

Little if any of the bitterness that this affair had generated had been apparent to me when I returned from Phnom Penh to Canberra in 1961. The Pocs, uncle and nephew, with their charming wives offered hospitality that mixed Cambodian charm with Gallic elegance. Poc Deuskomar seemed to have mellowed. The prejudice that he had expected had not been forthcoming and he appeared to enjoy the informality of life in the Australian capital. His English had improved strikingly and as a sign of the good living that he was experiencing he had become a little portly. There is no difficulty in remembering the last words he spoke to me in 1962, the last time I saw him before we met again four years later back in Phnom Penh. I was leaving the party he had given and we had all drunk well. He and I were probably both a little drunk as we chatted at the door. Had I noticed, he asked, that he was not so slim as he had once been. 'Ah,' he went on carefully enunciating his English, 'it's very good for the fucking, keeps the stomach against the woman!' I was not shocked, just a little surprised. This was not a side of Poc Deuskomar's character that he had revealed before. Certainly it left me with an image of him that was sharply altered once we met again in Phnom Penh.

No one will ever know the full details of the way in which Poc Deuskomar changed from the young Cambodian diplomat essaying Australian vulgarisms to the man who was ready to risk everything in pursuit of a revolution. In the course of four or five meetings during 1966 I gained some sense of his thinking about current developments in Cambodia, but much less of the personal journey that had led him to Communism. Poc's embrace of this ideology did not seem to mean that he had a highly developed grasp of Communist theory. Central to his decision, in my judgment, was a sense of total disgust with the system of government that prevailed in Cambodia, with the men who were ready to serve that system, and with Sihanouk for presiding over such a state.

Poc Deuskomar was no longer a Cambodian foreign service officer when I met him again in 1966. He had moved from diplomacy to the world of commerce and, in the nationalised economy that predominated in Cambodia by this time, he worked at the state-run National Credit Bank. Just why he had made this change he never explained explicitly, but the amount of time he spent dwelling on the experience of his uncle's ignominious recall in 1960 probably provides a partial explanation for the change. But only a partial explanation, since there is evidence that the change of employment may well have been made with another definite but ulterior motive in mind. When Poc Deuskomar finally did take to the *maquis* it was alleged that he and other left-wing associates at the National Credit Bank had been supplying money and medicines to insurgent forces in the countryside. At very least there seems to have been the possibility that Poc Deuskomar turned to banking for the opportunities it might give him of access to funds that could aid a slowly emerging revolutionary movement to which he was now committed.

For one thing is indeed much clearer as the result of the perspective afforded by the passage of time. This is the extent to which Cambodians, as opposed to foreigners, were aware of a slow but significant change in the nature of clandestine politics from the early 1960s onwards. Names that have become relatively well-known in the late 1970s were simply unknown to all but the most acute foreign observers, and not always to them, in the 1960s. Few, if any, who wrote about Cambodian politics in the 1960s had heard of Ieng Sary or Salot Sar. Yet these men and others formed a vitally important core group that had decided in the early 1960s that there was no longer any place for them in the overt politics of Sihanouk's Cambodia. Quite certainly a man such as Poc Deuskomar knew of the slow but steady trickle of men and women into the *maquis*. That he himself delayed in disappearing may have been the result of both personal and political factors. By the time he did choose to go into clandestine dissidence there could be little doubt as to the seriousness of the confrontation that was taking place between left-wing dissidents and the right-wing Cambodian army. But in 1966 it was still possible to have a last measure of uncertainty.

Cambodian society, in Poc Deuskomar's eyes, was rotten and only a radical left-wing solution could bring the necessary change that was required. It was when he moved away from this basic proposition that his viewpoint seemed less clear, or at any rate less informed by fact as opposed to hope. One judgment seemed extremely puzzling. Was it not correct, he suggested, that the left in Australia was growing more and more powerful with the likelihood of some form of 'victory' to which they could look forward? Although I had not been in my own homeland for nearly three years this did not seem to be a view that had much to do with reality. And it suggested to me that perhaps Poc Deuskomar really had done little more than enjoy himself while he was serving in Canberra. He spoke of his 'friends' who shared the same point of view as he did, and I wondered whom he meant. Later I was to discover that he spent a considerable amount of time with one of Sihanouk's French employees, Charles Meyer, a man of varying loyalties, but one who could certainly be described as being generally 'of the left'. And it transpired that Poc Deuskomar worked, in his spare time, with Chau Seng and played a part in writing the leftist-oriented editorials that appeared in the daily *La Dépêche*. This second piece of information still puzzles me for at our first meeting in 1966 Poc Deuskomar was at pains to denounce Chau Seng as a man who had only a superficial commitment to left-wing views. And unlike Poc Deuskomar Chau Seng never risked his life in the *maquis*.

Why Poc Deuskomar should have chosen to speak to me as he did I shall never know. Was he seeking a neutral sounding board? And was the apparent contradiction between his affirmation of a commitment and his continuing to operate in the world of overt politics real or the result of a deliberate wish to mystify? Without there ever being a way to be certain, I think the following judgments might be made. For the reasons already listed and for others that may never be known Poc Deuskomar had chosen the path of revolution. He recognised this, for to embrace Communism in Sihanouk's Cambodia could only mean opting for the ultimate goal of revolution. Having made this decision, however, the next step presented difficulties. In 1966, a would-be revolutionary had to ask how long should an effort be made to continue operating in the world of overt politics. In this regard Poc Deuskomar's decision to embrace Communism but not to disappear from Phnom Penh paralleled decisions made by the much better known left-wing politicians, Khieu Samphan, Hu Nim, and Hou Youn, who continued trying to work within the existing political system.

Time was running out for the men on the left, however, and 1966 was later to be seen as the last year when there could be any expectation that committed leftists could operate without grave personal risk in a Cambodia in which Sihanouk remained Chief of State. Elections held in September 1966 were followed by a steady swing to the right in Cambodian politics. When in April 1967 this move to the right was followed by the outbreak of rural insurgency in Battambang province Sihanouk began to listen more often to the advice of increasingly powerful right-wing politicians. It was these politicians who urged him to arrest Khieu Samphan, Hu Nim, Hou Youn and others who, they claimed, were behind the unrest in the countryside. Khieu Samphan and Hou Youn took the threat to their lives involved in such recommendations sufficiently seriously to flee from Phnom Penh in April. Hu Nim waited until October 1967 before he too faded into the *maquis*. We know this now, but at the time this was not the general belief as to what had taken place. In 1967 and for some years afterwards the assumption, among Cambodian and foreign observers alike, was that these three well-known left-wing Cambodians who disappeared so abruptly had, in fact, been murdered by Sihanouk's security police. Sihanouk claimed the men were still alive but most did not believe him. Considerable circumstantial evidence was cited to suggest that after having been seized and tortured the three men had been put to death in a particularly brutal fashion, one having been burnt to death by acid, the other two having been buried up to their necks in a field before being crushed to death under the tracks of a bulldozer. Kim Thit, a retired civil servant of great standing, and a senior member of the elite, asserted that he had seen conclusive documentation that this was what had happened.

This was the atmosphere in which Poc Deuskomar continued to maintain a risky existence in Phnom Penh. He had been publicly criticised by Sihanouk in 1966, along with Chau Seng, but perhaps because of his still powerful family and perhaps, too, because he was a much less prominent figure than the deputies who fled in 1967, he continued living in the capital, under surveillance but free from arrest. Finally, in July 1968, the time for departure had come and while travelling in Kompong Cham province, according to the authorities, he faded into the countryside.

Trying to provide an account of Poc Deuskomar's life once he had become a revolutionary presents real difficulties. At the time of his disappearance the Cambodian authorities appeared genuinely convinced that it was to some location in Kompong Cham province, north and east of Phnom Penh, that he had fled. But other sources tell a different story. In New York, in 1973, a Cambodian acquaintance who also knew Poc Deuskomar had an interesting story to tell me. Poc's apparent disappearance in Kompong Cham was nothing but a ruse, according to this man. He had felt sure that the security forces were about to arrest him, but he did not know where he should go in order to make contact with one of the groups making up the slowly growing revolutionary forces. In these circumstances and with the help of family and friends he had made his way secretly to a location near the port town of Kampot, on the southern coast. There he had waited for more than a year before being able to make contact with an insurgent group based in the rugged Kirirom plateau region west of Phnom Penh. Once associated with this group he rose rapidly to assume the position that brought his name once more into public discussion. He was appointed Deputy Minister for Foreign Affairs in the Royal Government of National Union that, under Sihanouk's nominal authority, publicly led the fight against the Lon Nol forces after the 1970 coup.

Ith Sarin, a defector from the Communist side while the war still raged in Cambodia, told a similar but different story. When Ith Sarin returned to Phnom Penh after nearly a year spent with the Communist led forces opposed to Lon Nol he sought to make his peace with the Phnom Penh authorities by providing them with a detailed account of his experiences. In the course of describing those leading insurgent figures whom he had encountered, Ith Sarin stated that when Poc Deuskomar disappeared from view in 1968 he had not gone into the countryside but, instead, had remained hidden in Phnom Penh.

Whether Poc Deuskomar hid in Phnom Penh or Kampot is academic. What is of interest is the suggestion that a man such as Poc Deuskomar should not know where to go when he no longer felt able to face the risk of living in Phnom Penh. This fact gives emphasis to at least two aspects of the development of the Cambodian Communist movement. First is the fact that it remained quite notably small until the onset of a brutal war created circumstances that enabled the Communist leaders to embark on a program of widescale recruitment. It was not enough to have made a commitment to Communism, or to want to be a revolutionary. It was also necessary to know where like-minded persons could be found, and Poc Deuskomar did not know this when he judged his time for flight, or at least for going into hiding, had come. The second point involves both comment and speculation. Cambodia's sparsely settled territory and the jungle and forest covered hills and mountains that ring the central plain offered ideal hiding places for the would-be insurgents as they waited for an opportunity to work for revolution. One can only speculate what life was like in these hiding places, screened from the outside world by the cover of vegetation and the real difficulties of access once the main roads are left behind. Life in such insurgent retreats cannot have been easy, especially not for a man such as Poc Deuskomar.

If life was hard, however, the final evidence that exists concerning his life in the *maquis* suggests that he thrived in his new role as an insurgent leader sharing the dangers of war and the discomforts of an existence lacking in the pleasures he had known in Phnom Penh. I make this observation on the basis of photographs I first saw in 1972, photographs that enabled me to conclude that not only was Poc Deuskomar alive, but that the same was also true of the three so-called missing deputies, Khieu Samphan, Hu Nim, and Hou Youn. When I called at the offices of the Royal Government of National Union in Paris, in 1972, I was among those who believed that Khieu Samphan and his colleagues had suffered the fate that Phnom Penh discussion ascribed to them. I changed my mind suddenly when I was shown a series of photographs in which not only they but Poc Deuskomar also appeared. There was simply no mistaking Poc Deuskomar or the 'missing deputies' with whom he was photographed. I did not know the others well, though I had seen them enough times in Phnom Penh to feel sure that these were the 'real' left-wing politicians whom I saw and not doubles. But above all, the authenticity of the pictures of Poc Deuskomar was beyond doubt. And what pictures they were. There was little if any sense of the photographs having been posed. Seated informally with his comrades Poc Deuskomar looked a happy man. He had lost weight so that he could never have ventured his Canberra witticism even if commitment to a new ideology would have permitted him to do so. He seemed finally, after the years of humiliation and then disgust in Sihanouk's Cambodia, to be content with what he was doing. These photographs provided the final confirmation of what I only dimly sensed in 1966, that for a man such as Poc Deuskomar the evils of Cambodian society as he and others like him perceived them could only be removed by recourse to radical solutions. Nothing less than total change could bring to an end a system that was totally rotten, totally corrupt, and totally offensive.

But something must have changed again for Poc Deuskomar. His name continued to appear on lists of the membership of the Royal Government of National Union until the defeat of the Lon Nol forces in April 1975. Then his name, as with so many others, was not recorded again. My first inquiries about this one Cambodian revolutionary whom I could claim to know in more than a passing fashion met with the suggestion that he was dead and that he, in fact, died well before final victory was achieved, probably in 1973. This widespread belief, it now appears, was wrong. At some stage, and before April 1975, Poc decided that he had had enough and left his comrades of the *maquis*. Had the brutal methods the Communists were already using to enforce their rule in areas under their control sickened him? I can only wonder, and wonder too if I will ever have the opportunity to ask him.

CHAPTER NINE

Portraits 4. An Older Prince

Nine months of work in the archives of Paris had left many questions about the history of nineteenth-century Cambodia unanswered, or only partly answered. My hope was that some issues would be resolved by consulting the documents that were held in the Phnom Penh archives. But I felt sure that there would be older Cambodians, particularly members of the royal family, who could add living flesh to what sometimes seemed like the bare dry bones of information culled from letters and reports. There was a memory I preserved from the period when I had worked in the embassy in Phnom Penh of Princess Pengpas Yukanthor, who had been born in the 1890s, and who was regarded as an authority on the history of the Cambodian royal family, particularly on its relations with the French colonial administration. This memory seemed particularly promising since her father, Prince Norodom Yukanthor, had been at the centre of one of the few great *causes célèbres* that had involved public acknowledgement of the deep antagonism existing between the ruler of Cambodia and the French. On returning to Phnom Penh in 1966 I made inquiries about seeing the princess. I was quietly told that she was now, sadly, senile.

Perhaps, a friend suggested, I should see Prince Norodom Montana. This prince was one of the most senior members of the Norodom branch of the royal family, the branch to which Sihanouk belonged, and his father had been perhaps the most prominent prince to fight against the French in the Cambodian Rising of 1885–86, the one major armed challenge to French control during colonial times. At sixty-four years of age, Norodom Montana was said to be clear-minded and quite happy to meet foreign visitors. But again there was disappointment. Prince Montana regretted the fact that few if any of his contemporaries, let alone the younger members of the royal family, took any serious interest in history. He now wished he had taken more interest in the stories he had heard in his youth and in the events he had himself witnessed. He feared that what had not already been recorded was probably forgotten. Apart from one interesting reference to there being a continuing tradition in the royal family that King Norodom had indeed been personally and closely involved in the planning for the 1885–86 Rising, something that the French had never been able to prove, there was little more that Prince Montana could offer.

Continuing inquiries finally brought their reward. I came to recognise that occasional anecdotes dredged by old men and women of the royal family from their memories of long-forgotten conversations with their parents and relatives sometimes did add up to a coherent picture of importance. Slowly, too, I found that there were descendants of the quasi-hereditary official families who had their oral traditions to offer as well. But most important of all, and after some little delay in being able to arrange the meeting, I met Prince Sisowath Entaravong. While I had known other members of his family I had not encountered this older prince before 1966. I knew much more about his dead brother, Prince Sisowath Youtevong, who had died in 1947 and had seemed in the immediate post-war period destined for a brilliant political career. Before Youtevong's death the nature of Cambodian politics had temporarily appeared likely to be different from what did occur once he was no longer alive and as the then King Sihanouk slowly grew to political maturity. For a brief period there seemed to be a real possibility of politics in Cambodia being genuinely democratic in character. If this comment begs many issues, there can be no denying that Prince Youtevong was, briefly, of great importance. But the knowledge I had of Youtevong did not extend to the details of his and Entaravong's ancestry, which gave them a particularly striking link with the past.

Their father, Prince Yubhiphan, was born in 1877. His father, Prince Essaravong, had been born nineteen years before that, in

1858, the son of Prince, later King Sisowath. What was striking about this situation was that at the time of Prince Sisowath Entaravong's birth in 1904 his father, then aged twenty-seven, had lived virtually his entire life under the reign of King Norodom I (reigned 1860-1904), and Entaravong's grandfather's life had begun before a French colonial presence had even been established in Cambodia. When I met Entaravong in 1966 I encountered someone whose ancestry, through only two preceding generations, reached back more than a century. In terms of the often short lives of Cambodians, even those who were more privileged as members of the royal family, this was striking. But what was even more striking was the fact that Entaravong proved to be a man of remarkable memory who could recount in detail what his father told him of the life he and his grandfather had led at Norodom's' court. Cross checking of what he recounted only served to underline the accuracy of his memory. I had been extraordinarily fortunate in finding a major and reliable source of oral history.

Through Prince Entaravong I gained a real sense of what life had been like at court. Had I heard of how King Ang Duong, who had died in 1860, had personally beaten his son and successor Norodom for failing to live up to the standards expected of him? Well, if I had seen such a suggestion, Entaravong remarked, it was certainly the case that Ang Duong's temper had still been a subject for discussion at the beginning of the present century and his beating of Norodom had been a tale often and gleefully told. Surely I knew something of the banquets Norodom had so greatly enjoyed before ill health in the late 1890s had cramped a taste for revelry that Entaravong's father had spoken of in awe? Listening to Entaravong talk was to be transported to the last decade of the nineteenth century. I was told of the things Prince Yubhiphan, Entaravong's father, had seen at the banquets Norodom had loved, those seemingly endless dinners that took place with the royal dancers providing a changing backdrop to the feasting on food and drink served in unstinted quantities.

Buddhism and its role in Cambodia had been one of the matters that so much of the French commentary I had read, both in archives and in printed works, had not covered. Once again, Prince

Entaravong had helpful observations to make. The French had been mistaken, he argued, to see any true political significance in the support that his great grandfather, King Sisowath, had given to the Thommayut sect in preference to the Mohanikay. Certainly some minor political capital might have been made out of King Sisowath's personal religious preferences, so that a knowing courtier might have advanced his position by showing devotion towards the reformed sect with its origins in Bangkok. But this was not a matter involving politics in any national sense, rather it was the never-ending petty political manoeuvring that had always been so characteristic of Cambodian court life. Perhaps such manoeuvring might have led to the advancement of one official rather than another since there was no doubt concerning Sisowath's deeply felt commitment to the Thommayut as opposed to the Mohanikay sect. Entaravong had his own sharp memory of how this preference could be shown. In 1915, when he was eleven, he 'took the robe' and spent four years in a monastery. The day he was to enter the monastery for the first time he with other young princes of the same age who were about to do the same went to pay his respects to King Sisowath, by then an old man of seventy-five. One by one the King asked the intending monks which monastery each was entering, indicating his approval as they named those linked to the Thommayut sect. When, however, one of Sisowath's grandsons indicated that he was entering a Mohanikay monastery the king flew into a towering rage that was only slightly mollified when the young prince begged him to remember that Sisowath's half-brother and predecessor as king, Norodom, had himself first taken the robe at a Mohanikay pagoda near the old capital of Oudong.

What Entaravong had to say of Buddhism in contemporary Cambodia stressed the differences between an era fifty or sixty years before and the situation that existed in 1966. It also provided confirmation of what others told me. As a Buddhist, Entaravong told me, he was disturbed by the extent to which there was an effort, he presumed at Sihanouk's direction, to try to have the Buddhist clergy play a political role in contemporary Cambodia. This was something new and dangerous, he argued. He was puzzled by the readiness of the leaders of the Mohanikay sect to agree to its taking place, but for whatever reason they and the monks of their order were speaking out on behalf of Prince Sihanouk and his policies. This, Entaravong insisted, was only one more sign of the decline that afflicted Cambodia. The economy was in ruins so that even Sihanouk had to admit the fact and to acknowledge that he had no ready answer to the problems that existed. As for Sihanouk's foreign policy, this was a matter Entaravong simply could not understand. To break diplomatic relations with the United States had left Cambodia exposed and he could see no reason why Sihanouk should trust the Vietnamese Communists' affirmations of friendship. There was no fundamental reason why Cambodia should be on bad terms with Thailand and there were many other Cambodians who were like him, Entaravong claimed, in feeling perfectly at home when they were in Bangkok and with Thai friends. Like so many others Entaravong had become highly critical of Sihanouk's rule and was, in 1966, prepared to say so.

That Sisowath Entaravong should have been a critic of Norodom Sihanouk was not, in itself, surprising. As I came to know him better I found that he like other members of his family retained a clear and affectionate memory of the late Prince Youtevong. And Prince Youtevong when he had been alive had made very apparent his opposition to the kind of personal regime that Sihanouk had finally instituted in Cambodia. What was less clear to me initially was the extent to which Entaravong's expressions of discontent with Sihanouk and his policies could be taken as representing something more than the views of one ageing man who looked back to what had for him been happier times. When I met and talked with him over a period of months about both the past and the present, this question arose, since Prince Entaravong seemed to be hinting that his opinions were broadly shared by other senior members of the royal family. In particular he spoke admiringly of Prince Sisowath Monireth as a man who saw many issues in the same terms as he did and as a leader who could rally Cambodians and lead them away from their present descent towards chaos.

It is not hard to be confused by the abundance of princes whose names dot the history of modern Cambodia, and it is easy to make many of them appear more important than they were. Under the rules that used to govern royalty in Cambodia there was a system of declining status according to the number of generations a man or woman was removed from a kingly ancestor. By the fifth generation a descendant of a king was no longer able to claim the title of prince or princess. When the size of the female households of such rulers as Norodom and Sisowath is taken into account it is easy to see why there should have been so many princes and princesses moving across the Cambodian stage. Indeed, the calculation was made in the early 1960s that, according to the rules that governed these matters, since all King Ang Duong's descendants (he had died in 1860) were eligible for succession to the Cambodian throne, this meant there were in excess of four hundred possible contenders for the office of king. But the question remained: How important was the royal family in Cambodian politics by 1966?

There can be no absolute answer. During the period of colonial control and up to Sihanouk's accession to the throne in 1941 the French had always placed heavy emphasis on what they saw as the dynastic divisions existing in the royal family and on the feuds they saw fuelled by these divisions. The French also saw these feuds as having political risks attached to them. At the heart of the feuds was the succession that had taken place in 1904 when old King Norodom ended a long life of bitter opposition to French efforts to exert almost total control over his country. When Norodom died he was succeeded, as the result of French pressure, not by one of his many sons but by his half-brother, Sisowath. From that time until Sihanouk mounted the throne in 1941 the Norodom branch of the royal family had felt cheated. When Sisowath died in 1927 a member of the Sisowath branch, his son Monivong, succeeded him and the Norodoms continued to feel aggrieved. But it was the Sisowaths' turn to lose out in 1941 and, as the result of French interference stemming largely from their fear that Monivong's eldest surviving son would be too independent, the young Norodom Sihanouk was unexpectedly placed on the throne.

So there was a background of family discord that was frequently matched to intrigue. The royal family was large, factious, and in 1966 still very visible. When it came to national politics, however,

the number of princes who were of real importance was probably
very small. In speaking admiringly of Prince Sisowath Monireth,
Entaravong had certainly named one of those who, at very least,
could be regarded as potentially a political leader. Prince
Monireth as King Monivong's eldest surviving son was a very
senior prince. As Monivong's son he was also Sihanouk's uncle
since Monireth's sister, Kossamak, was Sihanouk's mother.
Monireth had chosen a military career and had served with the
Foreign Legion in North Africa before the Second World War.
It was widely believed that he had expected to succeed his father,
but when the French choice fell on Sihanouk he had kept his
silence. To a considerable extent he had also retreated from public
life and only occasionally did he agree to become involved in
political affairs. On those occasions he showed himself to be above
factional politics and on one famous occasion he resigned from
being a minister in one of Sihanouk's cabinets because of the lack
of cooperation he had received in his efforts to wipe out corruption. If, in 1966, I understood Entaravong correctly he was
suggesting that the time might be coming when Monireth would
have to return to the political arena once again.

Then and now this judgment seemed unrealistic. In 1966 Prince
Monireth was still only fifty-seven years old and there was no
doubt that he continued to be regarded with respect both for his
high royal status and for his general probity. But he had long
since ceased to play an active part in politics. Although it seemed
likely he shared the views of men such as Entaravong and was
concerned about the economic decline in which the country seemed
gripped and worried about the policies that Sihanouk pursued
towards the Vietnamese Communists, there seemed little reason
to believe that he had the necessary political links that would make
him an effective leader even if this were a role he wished to play.
Being a senior prince would aid him if he was also a politician,
but being a prince was not enough by itself. Monireth did not
return to public life.

If Entaravong's estimations concerning Prince Monireth were
lacking in realism he was, as a prince, expressing a point of view
that said in part, that any alternative to Prince Sihanouk's

government, particularly one that was ready to push Sihanouk aside, could only enhance its claim to legitimacy by having a member of the royal family associated with it.

I saw Prince Entaravong briefly in 1967 and then not again until February 1970. By then the situation in Cambodia had become critical and Sihanouk's deposition was a mere six weeks away. As he reviewed developments Entaravong was close to despair. But he did see one reason for hope. A prince had come forward who was ready to be a politician and whose royal prestige could aid in implementing policies that ran counter to those pursued by Sihanouk. The only cause for concern was whether this prince yet had enough supporters to press through the urgent measures that were needed without delay. The man of whom he spoke was Prince Sisowath Sirik Matak, a long-time critic of Sihanouk who had paid for his criticism by having to occupy a series of appointments abroad that had kept him from playing a role in domestic politics. For men such as Entaravong, and for many others of a conservative cast of mind whether princes or not, Sirik Matak's return appeared to herald the possibility of a fresh start and to offer the prospect of a royal politician whose policies would be in tune with the interests and desires of the segment of society from which he came. Eight years later the bitter irony of this estimation is all too clear. Whatever his knowledge of the past, Entaravong was sadly out of touch with many of the most important realities of the present. There could be no return to a simpler past in which royal status guaranteed success. The hopes for salvation he saw in Sirik Matak were meaningless beyond the short-term achievement of seeing Sihanouk removed from power. For brave and probably largely uncorrupt though he was, Prince Sirik Matak was not a man of notable political skill and the problems that Cambodia faced once it became engulfed in the Second Indochinese War were not of a character that had much to do with issues of royal status. This was the lesson that Sirik Matak died for in 1975. It was the lesson that Sihanouk was humiliatingly to learn when he returned to Phnom Penh after the Communist victory in 1975 and found himself under house arrest. As for Prince Entaravong, kindly and knowledgeable conservative that he was, he may no longer have hoped that royal status was the key to power by the time of the Communist victory of April 1975. But like so many others he made an even more serious mistake. He did not believe Cambodia's new rulers would set out to destroy even the remnants of existing society. So he remained in Phnom Penh. Then, with hundreds of thousands of others, he disappeared as part of the forced mass evacuation of the city. There was a rumour of his being alive in late 1975, and then nothing more.

CHAPTER TEN

Academic Questions

So far as I can tell only two foreigners worked for sustained periods in the Cambodian archives after the French had granted independence to the country in 1953. One was Charles Meyer, whose role in Cambodian politics deserves the fuller attention it receives in Chapter 14, and I was the other. A small number of foreign scholars did, it is true, penetrate into the archives building to consult newspapers, but Meyer and I as foreigners, and one Cambodian scholar, Sarin Chhak were the only persons to spend any significant period of time leafing through the yellowing manuscripts housed not far from the small hill, or *phnom*, that gave the Cambodian capital its name. Using the archives was a fascinating experience and one that was vital to the completion of my research. It was also an experience that, once again, could not be divorced from the political overtones which intruded into every aspect of Cambodian life in 1966.

Looking back I am amazed at the optimism with which I travelled to Cambodia in the hope of finding archival material that would be relevant to my study of the impact made by the French colonial presence from the early 1860s to a period towards the end of the first decade of the twentieth century when events following the death of King Norodom signalled a major change in the nature of the Franco–Cambodian relationship. I hoped I would find material of interest but I had absolutely no certainty that I would. Nor, in retrospect, had I fully appreciated how great would be the contrast between life in Phnom Penh as a junior diplomat and life in the same city as a rather older-than-usual graduate student who was distinctly short of money. Apart from one bout of serious illness with amoebic dysentery that had ended with my losing nearly thirty pounds of weight and with a period of hospitalisation in Bangkok, the time I spent with the embassy had been more than agreeable. As the reality of my changed status became more and more apparent to me during my first few weeks in Phnom Penh in 1966, so did I remember ever more vividly how cosseted I had been before. It was difficult as I tried, in the rain, to find a *cyclopousse* not to dwell on the TR-2 sports car, painted in British Racing Green, that I had sadly left behind in 1961. And how could I forget the interest and absurdity of appearing at state functions clad in a white sharkskin suit, a garb that managed to make the Phnom Penh Diplomatic Corps look like a convention of rather seedy Italian ice cream vendors. As I debated whether I could afford a large bottle of beer at the end of the day, or would have to settle for a small one, I cast back envious thoughts to the pleasures of duty-free scotch, to the series of 'black velvet' parties that I had held in the closing months of my posting, and to the highly successful first importation of Australian wine into Cambodia—highly successful in esteem, that is, for these were first-class Hunter Valley reds and whites, but in terms of breakage a disaster for the bottles had been so poorly packed.

There was no denying that I had come down in the world in terms of my accommodation. In place of the flat rented by the Australian Government I occupied one of the very few unairconditioned rooms still left in the old Hôtel le Royal. To have found such a room was, in fact, a real coup since for something less than three American dollars a day I had a room in Phnom Penh's 'Raffles'. And I could use the hotel's swimming pool. The only problem was that, apart from breakfast, I could not afford to eat the excellent food provided by the hotel's restaurant. In one of the more convincing and mysterious demonstrations of the efficiency of international banking I paid for all of this with cheques drawn on my American bank in Ithaca, New York. Hotel bills had to be paid in hard currency rather than in Cambodian riels so my cheques, I was assured, were entirely welcome. And indeed, some three to four weeks after I handed my cheque to the hotel cashier the amount would be debited from my account with the Tompkins County Trust Company; no matter at all that Cambodia and the United States did not have diplomatic relations. To all these benefits was added the fact that the hotel was less than two minutes walk from the archives.

It took some little time to gain admission to the archives. The problems were varied. The head of the National Library under whose jurisdiction the archives fell could not understand why anyone, most particularly a foreigner, should want to look at old documents. I still am not sure that my efforts to explain why someone interested in Cambodia's history should want to examine documents were successful. Cambodia's history had already been written, he assured me, and the library had the books to prove it. As politely as possible I persisted. If the head of the National Library checked would he not find that almost all of the books that had been written about Cambodia's history dated from many years ago, and even more important had they not been written by Frenchmen? What I wanted to do was to take a fresh look at what had happened during the long reign of King Norodom I, the great grandfather of Prince Sihanouk, and a man who had so often been unfairly denigrated by French officials. Whether persistence, the hint of flattery of Sihanouk's ancestor, or the sheer unexpectedness of my request carried the day I shall never know. Suddenly, however, I was told I could examine the archives.

I had hoped there might be something of interest; I found a treasure trove. Not that examining this wealth of important papers was a straightforward operation. No one, not even those who worked in the building housing the archives, knew anything about the documents that were stored on the three floors of the repository. What was more, I already knew before I went to Phnom Penh that in the closing stages of the French presence in Cambodia, as had also happened in Vietnam and Laos, a team of archivists from metropolitan France had removed a substantial quantity of documents with the intention of creating a new *dépot* for colonial archives in Aix-en-Provence. Clearly luck and ingenuity would be needed if the archives were to be used to any purpose. And luck and ingenuity would be needed between the hours of 7am and 1.30pm, for outside of those hours, Saturday included, the archives were closed.

My work in the archives began in mid-April and the contrast

between the working conditions I had known when I had been with the embassy and those I now encountered was sharp. Even before eight o'clock in the morning during April and May the building housing the archives had become stiflingly hot. It seemed to be policy not to open more than the bare minimum of windows and there were no ceiling fans. As the day progressed so did the heat and the humidity become greater. Towards the end of April the temperature rose above one hundred degrees Fahrenheit day after day while the air was saturated with humidity. I sat at the small space that had been cleared for me with sweat dripping off my elbows, my shirt and trousers sticking to me, and wrote and wrote.

My necessary stroke of luck came fairly quickly, and perhaps involved some ingenuity. I had begun my work in the Phnom Penh archives on exactly the same basis as if I had still been working in the archives in Paris. There was a catalogue showing the boxes of archives that had once been held and the subjects of the files contained in each box. Having noted a box or file that appeared interesting I requested a member of the staff to bring it to me. It soon became apparent that this procedure was regarded as being as troublesome to the staff as it was time-consuming and frustrating for me. More often than not the item I requested would be missing, perhaps mislaid, possibly transferred to France. And even when the requested item was found the search to locate it could take up to an hour. Might it be possible, I tentatively inquired, for me to look through the storage areas myself and so, perhaps, find whether there might be concentrations of files dealing with periods and subjects that interested me? If these could be located the archives staff would be spared the tedium of having to search for the material I had requested. To my amazement this request was granted.

From early May for a period of nearly a month I was able to roam the storage areas of the archives and make my own selection of documents to be taken downstairs to be studied and recorded. This was luck beyond anything I had expected. And it revealed the conditions under which the archives were being stored, which was worse than anything I might have imagined. The ground floor of the archives building was cluttered and crowded, most particularly with the stacks of recent newspapers that were stored there. But it was relatively clean. The two floors above were another matter entirely. Dust was everywhere. More seriously, termites were rampant and their nests were built among the boxes that lined the wooden shelves and in many cases on top of old minute books and registers. Birds nests were common and as I walked along the narrow passages birds would suddenly dart from their nests flapping past me to find some way to the open air outside. Time after time I opened boxes to find that termites had destroyed part or all of the papers inside. History was being reduced to dust.

But still some wonderful finds remained, documents that I had not found in France, nor had really expected to find in Cambodia. As I searched through the dusty shelves, sometimes having to brush feathers and bird droppings from the covers of old letter books, I found the minutes of the Cambodian Council of Ministers, with the proceedings recorded in both French and Cambodian. No less interesting were the volumes that recorded in manuscript the letters exchanged between the King of Cambodia and the French *Résident Supérieur* in the first decade of the twentieth century. Then there were the personal dossiers of the senior Cambodian officials who had worked as part of the Cambodian administration while having to sustain constant pressure from the French to serve the colonial power's interests rather than those of their ruler. These files had not been catalogued so that hours had to be spent in the hot unventilated upper floors of the archives building sorting through apparently endless numbers of boxes to find material that related to important officials rather than to messengers and clerks.

All of this had to be done in an atmosphere of doubt, and sometimes open suspicion. More than once I was queried about what I was doing. How could the dossier I was examining that gave the details of a man's career as a senior Cambodian official in the late nineteenth century be 'History'? I would always try to explain, but I never had much conviction that I had succeeded. If I had achieved no more success in the archives than that resulting from the one month of free access to the storage area the trip to Cambodia would have been justified. My understanding of the period of history I was studying was transformed. Trends I had guessed at on the basis of work in Paris were now confirmed by detailed documentation. The true tragedy of the final years of King

Norodom's life became sharply apparent and the readiness of his
half-brother and successor, Sisowath, to bow to virtually any
French demand was given even greater confirmation. The Cambodian officials whom I had encountered in the documents held in
Paris became rounded figures as I read of their progression through
the ranks of the royal service and saw their merits discussed in
the minutes of the Council of Ministers.

Almost exactly one month after this period of unrestricted access
to the storage areas began I received the news I had always feared
would finally come. I was not, under any circumstances, the head
of the National Library informed me, ever to enter the storage
areas of the archives again. I made no protest for it was clear
that no effect would be achieved and I already suspected that my
presence in the archives was seen by some as a nuisance, at best,
and a threat, at worst.

Even though I could no longer roam the storage areas I was
still able to make requests for dossiers and sometimes these could
be found. It was a lucky dip form of procedure. What appeared
from the catalogue cards to be a promising box might contain
nothing more than a series of weapons returns sent into Phnom
Penh by the French *résidents*, or district officers, in the various
administrative divisions of the country. But the reverse happened
often enough for my spirits to remain high. One unexpected find
involved a long and interesting report on Pailin, the gem mining
town in western Cambodia I visited in August 1966. It came out
of a box that had given no suggestion that such a document was
inside. A box containing documents on the French medical service
in Cambodia that I nearly did not bother to request had among
other papers of no interest to me a detailed journal kept by a
French army doctor during the Rising of 1885–86. His account
of the medical problems faced by the French troops made clearer
than ever before the costs the colonial administration had paid to
regain control of the country. Not everything that I found was
of a sort to find a place in my dissertation. Yet the documents
I sifted were often invaluable for the sense of period they contained.
There was a macabre fascination about the instructions given for
the execution of a criminal carried out in a small provincial town
a little way from Phnom Penh. Here was death reduced to routine:
so many soldiers were to be present to keep order among the crowd

that would gather to witness the event; the official in charge was to make sure that sufficient sand was scattered about the base of the guillotine to absorb the blood that would flow once the blade had severed the criminal's head from his body. It was striking when one thought of the existence of fundamental ethnic antipathy between the Cambodians and the Vietnamese to note that the executioner, the man responsible for the 'high works' in the sinister French phrase, was a Vietnamese.

I spent the whole of July 1966 in Vietnam. When I returned to Phnom Penh it was easy to slip back into the routine of mornings spent in the archives, of waiting and hoping that a box of documents might exist to match an entry on a catalogue card, and of finding, increasingly, that more often than not the files I wanted to look at could not be found. By August it was the middle of the rainy season and sitting in the archives was a much more comfortable affair. But the greater physical comfort was not matched by the atmosphere in which I worked. If I had felt there was suspicion before, something more was present now. It did not seem to be personal hostility towards me. Rather the archives staff gave the impression that they feared that my using the archives might in some fashion cause them difficulties. And as I moved about Phnom Penh I began to hear gossip about my work in the archives, the classic 'one says that' of French rumour mongering. 'Someone' was saying that the authorities might be displeased by some of the information I had found in the archives, that it might reflect on the character of Sihanouk's ancestors. 'Someone' was saying that Charles Meyer, as the person in Phnom Penh who felt himself to be the unchallenged authority on Cambodian history, was unhappy to think of someone else, particularly an Anglo-Saxon, knowing of material that he had not seen himself. It was worrying to an extent, but I was not planning to stay much longer in Phnom Penh and I was fairly certain that I had consulted most of the material that was important to me. I did not take the matter too seriously.

I should have, for by the end of August I was barred from entering the archives altogether. On reflection I have to judge that it was perhaps my own fault. In August 1966 Phnom Penh conversation turned constantly to the subject of Cambodia's borders with Vietnam. The confusion stemming from the disputed position of Thlok Trach, the village that had been attacked twice by American aircraft at the end of July and the beginning of August, had only intensified Prince Sihanouk's desire to have the countries of the world declare their respect for Cambodia's existing borders. In his speeches Sihanouk dwelt on the lessons of the past and drew attention to the way that Cambodia had lost territory to its neighbours as the result of conquest and then, in the nineteenth and twentieth centuries, because of the French favouring the administration in southern Vietnam. His ancestor, King Norodom, Sihanouk added, had always resisted the French when they sought to make border changes, even if this was to no avail.

What Sihanouk said concerning his great grandfather was essentially correct. Norodom's concern to preserve Cambodia's territorial integrity was a consistent pattern of his life. With one exception. Towards the end of his life, with ill health sapping his energy and more than three decades of resisting French pressure taking their toll, Norodom was pressed to make a decision concerning Cambodia's northern borders with the modern state of Laos. On this one occasion he told the French official who sought to involve him in discussion of the problem that he did not care. The French were in charge and they could take whatever decision they thought necessary. Norodom was old, tired, and exasperated when he took this position and it was hardly a serious qualification of his previous behaviour. My mistake was to refer to the incident in public.

There had been plenty in the archives of both Paris and Phnom Penh that might have made good dinner party chatter during the months I spent in Cambodia had I chosen to use the information. The tension between Norodom and his half-brother Sisowath was one such item that would have surely excited interest. The sexual antics of the unmarried princesses of the royal family were another topic that undoubtedly would have commanded attention. For-bidden to marry unless it was to a prince of the same rank, the unmarried princesses used to smuggle 'men of the people' into their bedrooms. But discretion suggested that however well these anecdotes might be received Phnom Penh was not the place for recounting the more pointed or light hearted side of historical research. Quite seriously, why I made a different judgment in relation to the border question remains unclear to me. I like to think that it was not a case of my having had one glass of wine too many at the lunch where my indiscretion took place. Possibly I was unconsciously letting down my defences as I knew that a long and sometimes difficult period of research was going to end shortly. And perhaps, also, I succumbed to that terrible temptation that besets every graduate student. Having become in a very real sense *the* expert on a topic it is almost impossible to pass up the opportunity of demonstrating one's expertise. As discussion of the borders took place and as reference was made to Norodom's role in the past I spoke of the instance recorded in the Phnom Penh archives when Norodom had not fought the French in relation to his country's boundaries.

Two days later I learnt that I was no longer able to consult the Phnom Penh archives.

What had happened? And why? I was never able to establish the full details, but I think what had happened was this: The lunch at which I had so incautiously made my remarks had been a sizeable gathering at which a number of French military officers were present. They were from the French training mission that had functioned in Cambodia ever since independence. One of these men, I later found, was an intelligence officer who had served as an adviser to the Cambodia army for many years. It was he, I think, who retailed my reference to what I had seen in the archives to Charles Meyer, the Frenchman who served as one of Sihanouk's principal speech writers and who, as a cartographer by training, advised the Prince on border matters. Armed with the information of my indiscreet remarks Meyer appears to have persuaded the head of the National Library to deny me access to the archives. He was later to assure me that he was doing all that he could to have the prohibition against entry removed.

A curious feature of the affair was that it stopped at the level it did. The scrap of information I had discovered did not really affect the broad facts of the historical record showing Norodom as a staunch defender of Cambodia's territory. But if my discovery of this minor inconsistency, coupled with the fact that Sihanouk venerated Norodom's memory, was sufficient to give offence, how was it that I did not receive a more official rebuke, or a request to leave the country? The answer to this question lay in personal rather than official considerations.

As soon as I had arrived in Phnom Penh in April 1966 I had made arrangements to see Charles Meyer. I knew that with his long experience of Cambodia he had become an almost unmatched repository of information concerning the country. At some levels his knowledge was that of a real expert. At other levels, and this was so in terms of Cambodia's history in the nineteenth century, his knowledge was patchy and sometimes little more than un-documented gossip. He had used the archives, but never in a systematic fashion. I found it striking that it was after I told him of some interesting material I had found relating to the 1885–86 Rising that the documents in question, with his politically inspired gloss accompanying them, appeared in the small journal he published dealing with various aspects of Cambodia. I had called to see him over the months and told him in some detail of the kind of information I was finding but I had failed to recognise that Meyer had come to see me as a rival. He resented the challenge, as he saw it, of someone else gaining a deeper knowledge than he had of one aspect of Cambodia's past.

I have said that I think this is what happened. I cannot be sure that Meyer was responsible for my being denied the luxury of moving through the storage areas. But in fact I have little doubt that his was the influence that led to the uncomfortable atmosphere that I encountered when I returned to use the archives in August. I know he engineered my final exclusion after I was foolish enough to speak as I did at the lunch, for he spoke of having done so to a mutual acquaintance.

These events had little significance in the broader scheme of Cambodia's increasingly difficult domestic and international posi-tion. Nevertheless, what occurred in relation to my efforts to use the Phnom Penh archives says something about Cambodia in 1966. Nothing was untouched by politics or manoeuvring in that year. A Frenchman such as Meyer found it imperative to take a position about a 'rival' in the field. For in an atmosphere of increasing polarisation there could be nothing that was not political. The reaction to my research was a significant testimony to this fact.

CHAPTER ELEVEN

Cambodia seen from the East

Even in more peaceful times to travel from Phnom Penh to Saigon was to move from one world into another. Phnom Penh had its Chinese quarter, as raucous and bustling as any in Southeast Asia. Additionally, there were sections of the city where members of the Vietnamese immigrant community predominated. But as a whole there was no doubting the city's Cambodian character, something that had as much to do with the pace of life as with the distinctive architecture of the royal palace or the bright yellow, green, and blue tiles on the roofs of the dozens of Buddhist pagodas. Cambodia and its people represented the most easterly extension of Indian cultural influence and as such the land and the people were in sharp contrast to what lay across the border in Vietnam. The journey to Saigon involved crossing a cultural divide for the society that existed in Vietnam was profoundly affected by Chinese influence. Not that Vietnam was or is a 'little China'. That was a mistake that foreign observers had too often made and were continuing to make in 1966 as Hanoi was seen as merely an extension of Peking. Nevertheless, it was impossible to move from Phnom Penh to Saigon without realising how great were the differences existing between the populations of the two cities.

Phnom Penh in the mid-1960s had a population of about five hundred thousand. Saigon's population at the same time was probably well in excess of one and a half million, and growing all the time. Planned by the French as a rival to Singapore, Saigon's centre had the slightly contrived appearance of a big city. When I had spent a month there working in the archives in late

103

1962 and early 1963 the elegance of its buildings and of its population had already faded sharply by contrast with the city I had first seen in 1959. But enough sense of the past elegance remained to see why the city had exercised a fascination over so many of those who had lived there. In 1966 one had to search very hard to find any remnants of either elegance or charm.

The change from 1963 to 1966 was apparent even before my aircraft landed at Saigon's airport. By 1966 Tan Son Nhut airport was the second busiest airport in the world, surpassed only by Chicago's O'Hare for the volume of traffic flowing in and out each day. From the aircraft a panoramic view showed the tightly packed urban concentration that made up Saigon and its twin city of Cholon, which was the heart of the Chinese settlement in southern Vietnam. Saigon did not straggle into the countryside. The edges of the city were sharply defined, stopping suddenly where the vivid green of the rice lands surrounding the urban mass began. The air above the city was thick with pollution so that from a distance it appeared that the closely massed buildings lay beneath a gigantic yellowish-brown dome. The pollution was so thick that it had semblance of solidity making it appear much more than a cloud. The reason for this pollution became apparent after I had passed through the tediously protracted customs and immigration procedures. Saigon was a city locked in a permanent traffic jam. Giant American army GMC trucks ground along bumper to bumper. The squat little blue and white taxis, most probably manufactured in France fifteen or even twenty years before, somehow managed to slip from one stream of traffic to another looking as much like strangely shaped water beetles as could any land locked form of transportation. Everywhere there was the splutter and whine of two-wheeled vehicles powered by two-stroke motors, pouring their foul exhausts into the atmosphere in such quantities that the once graceful trees along the city's roads were barely alive and had ceased to bring forth new leaves. The Honda company of Japan had achieved such staggering commercial success in its sales of motorcycles that the Vietnamese word to cover all of these vehicles, of whatever make, was now *xe-honda*.

A newcomer to Saigon had the senses battered by the sights and sounds of the city. I arrived during the great garbage strike of 1966 and filth and rubbish of all sorts lay along the main streets of the city, sometimes piled four feet high, smelling more repulsive as each day passed. Silence seemed unknown. The room I worked in at the back of the National Library was screened from the traffic noise of Gia Long street, but nowhere was free from the distinctive staccato engine note of the helicopters that passed constantly over the city. At night, staying in a house a mile and a half from the city's centre, the luxury of an airconditioner could not drown out the sound of artillery barrages being fired from batteries set on the defence perimeter. Wherever one went in the downtown areas there were people, droves of people, pushing and bustling, crowding off the footpaths and on to the streets. The austerity of Phnom Penh contrasted with Saigon's profusion of stalls along Le Loi street and down past what had once been the flower market and now selling black market goods of every kind. Bottles of Chivas Regal sat beside army issue mosquito repellent. It was possible to buy every item of American uniform, from boots to underpants, with the latter still in their Department of Defence wrappers. President Lyndon Johnson's policy of escalation was in full swing and Saigon was paying the price in many ways.

This was not the way in which many saw the situation. Not, certainly, the American heavy equipment operator who shared a room with me and five others in a seedy hotel for five American dollars a night. He assured me that he did not care how long the war went on. A Texan, he trusted his Texan president, and besides where else in the world was he going to find a job like his present one that paid him fifteen hundred dollars a month? The bar owners whose establishments had robbed Tu Do street of its once genuine charm did not mind. Nor did some of the American army headquarters staff. They would tell a visitor of the job that was being done, and of the victory that was assured now that America was seriously involved in the war. In 1966 there was still much optimism among Westerners in southern Vietnam, not just among Americans. And one of the notable features of this prevalence of optimism and the pressure-filled pace of life was a readiness, even a compulsion, to talk at length and in the greatest detail about the strategy and the tactics of the war. Saigon was a forum for constant debate and discussion of the war as well as being a city of rumours exceeding even those of Phnom Penh in volume and shrill improbability.

When I was not working in the archives or at the National Library I listened with fascination to the advocates of this war and to the prophets of success. Having come to Saigon from Cambodia at first it seemed to me that here was not only another world, but one in which Cambodia's presence adjacent to Vietnam was simply ignored. Apparently, Vietnam, too, was only important in some larger, global context. Some of the opinions concerning the rectitude of American policy were, to me, of an order to have dazzled the casuists of the medieval church. I recorded in my journal the arguments of one of the most able of these advocates who began his sophisticated assessment by partially discounting the 'domino theory'. The United States, his argument ran, was really fighting the Soviet Union's battle by coming to the aid of the Saigon regime. It was doing this because the American commitment to the government in Saigon was demonstrating to the leadership in Hanoi that peaceful co-existence was the answer to world ideological differences. He did not see the northern Vietnamese leaders as tools of Peking. In many ways the revolutionary commitment of the Vietnamese Communists was ahead of that of the Chinese. But if southern Vietnam was not 'held' the resultant unified Vietnam would pose not just the threat of neighbouring countries falling like dominoes but rather the potential for change in countries such as Thailand and Malaysia —Cambodia was not mentioned—that would not be in the West's general interest.

As for the military and political situation, there was certainly no end in sight to the war and the southern Vietnamese political structure remained fragile. But matters were improving and as American force levels rose to perhaps half a million there would be significant improvement in the countryside by the end of 1967.

More than twelve years later it is easy to see the irony in so much of this intelligent man's appreciation of what was happening. The expected significant improvement that was to come by the end of 1967 was, to the extent that it ever existed, largely wiped out by the Vietnamese Communists' costly but politically highly effective Tet Offensive of early 1968. In the longer view the commitment of the United States and a small number of her allies to supporting the regime in Saigon ensured rather than prevented the spread of full-scale war into Cambodia and Laos and the ultimate triumph of Communist regimes in those two countries. In 1966 however, all was not optimism in Vietnam. As I travelled from the delta regions to the old imperial capital of Hué I began to meet the pessimists and the men who fell somewhere between the extremes of fervent belief and unqualified gloom. As I travelled I finally heard men speak of the war in Vietnam as it related to Cambodia.

As the days passed it became clear to me that despite all the brave words and convictions of progress there was an air of barely suppressed frustration widespread in the ranks of the American military in Vietnam. If they had believed what their president had told them in February 1966, that it was 'vitally important to every American family that we stop the Communists in South Vietnam', then the passage of four months had already demonstrated how difficult this task was going to be. The basic fact had to be faced: the Communists had not been 'stopped'. Whether or not they were winning depended on how the word 'win' was defined, but in 1966 there were some men in Vietnam who had begun to make the same sort of appreciation of developments as that later published by Henry Kissinger before he became Secretary of State. In a situation in which conventional forces are confronting insurgents the fact that the conventional forces are unable to 'win' means, fundamentally, that the insurgents are achieving victory. Even so it would be wrong to say that morale was low among the American officers and men with whom I spoke. In Saigon there was nothing like the scenes that could later be witnessed daily as morale plunged and discipline disintegrated. By 1970 a visitor to Saigon could see GIs addicted to heroin seeking out fixes in the side streets of the city. A visitor could also witness repeated instances of orders ignored or barely obeyed. And the same visitor could hear that the Marines of I Corps, in the north of the country, had been badly affected by drugs, while the deplorable discipline of the 9th Division in the delta was a matter for common comment. These things were yet to come. But if morale remained high so was the level of frustration.

There was frustration at a range of levels. At the tactical level the refusal of main force Communist units to respond to American thrusts in an expected fashion led to bizarre and costly measures being adopted on a routine basis. Units and sections of units were deliberately being committed as decoys in the hope of their being able to draw the Communists into battle. Only days after I arrived in Saigon there was one of these increasingly common engagements in the Mekong delta during which the Americans lost many troops killed as five armoured personnel carriers and several helicopters were destroyed after being sent into a known Communist area as decoys. When the decoys had flushed the enemy into making a response the Americans could then bring their massive firepower to bear. But the frustration remained and the costs were high. Far to the north of the delta, in Hué, I learnt how amazed were veteran Australian soldiers at the tactics followed by the American allies. Tough, long-serving warrant officers who had fought in Korea and Malaysia had nothing but admiration for the raw courage displayed by the Marines, but they could not believe that men should be asked to fight as they did. In order to make contact with the enemy they were led straight into the fight, suffering unnecessarily high casualties and once they had withdrawn, achieving little if any long-term effect.

Frustration existed on the level of strategy, even grand strategy, and this was when I started to hear reference to Cambodia. Fundamental to the thinking of many American planners, both military and civil, was the conviction that the Communists could not continue to fight in southern Vietnam if action was taken against their sanctuaries in Cambodia and Laos. If one accepted this basic premise, (and I did not) that the war in Vietnam could in fact be 'won', then it was difficult to deny that there was a measure of logic to the argument that the war should be carried to the sanctuaries. The trouble with this logic was the extent to which it departed from both political and military reality. It was based on an unreal premise. The unreal premise was that the Vietnamese Communists would finally accept the existence of two Vietnamese states. This was not an issue of morality or of the hopes and desires of the 'Free World'. It was simply a question of fact. The language of American discussion of Vietnamese affairs showed how persistent and deep-rooted the existence of this premise was. References to the 'South Vietnamese nation' and insistence upon 'North Vietnamese infiltration' demonstrated how so many Americans simply had not grasped the basic realities of Vietnamese political life.

In accepting this false premise the possibility of ending the war by striking against Vietnamese troops *outside* the territorial limits of southern Vietnam came to be seen as an increasingly attractive strategy. By 1966, moreover, both Laos and Cambodia had a vital part to play in the plans of the Vietnamese Communists. There will probably never be agreement concerning just how vital this part was. Without any doubt the trail system winding southwards through Laos was one of the essential supply routes for Communist forces fighting south of the seventeenth parallel. The situation in Cambodia was more complicated. Areas of Cambodia's eastern border regions were used as supply and staging areas for Vietnamese Communist troops; but for how many troops and what areas were used? The situation in 1966 was certainly not as clear-cut as it became by 1970. The gift of food that Sihanouk gave to representatives of the National Liberation Front in April 1966 was intended by the Prince to be a symbol of Cambodia's sympathy for the Communist cause, but it also represented the visible part of a much larger trade in rice and goods of every kind that went on between Cambodia and southern Vietnam. Whatever the debates concerning magnitudes and details, areas of eastern Cambodia were in 1966 inextricably involved in the Vietnam War.

In these circumstances, the falsely founded logic proceeded, the war should be carried to the enemy wherever he was. Listening to the advocacy that the war be carried into Cambodia I was amazed. Were these colonels and majors, were the short-term contract men from the Agency of 'Revolutionary Development' projects, seriously suggesting that a war which was already showing itself to be unwinnable in southern Vietnam could be brought to an end by making it wider in scope? Where would these strikes against Cambodia and Laos end—five miles beyond the border, twenty miles, fifty miles? Even more to the point, in uncomplicated military terms how many more troops would be needed to ensure that the areas attacked would not lapse into being sanctuaries once American troops drew back into Vietnam? As I dared to ask these questions I found that these men, deeply frustrated about the lack of progress in southern Vietnam, were indeed serious in their suggestions.

It was hard to believe, and hard to take their seriousness

seriously. Advocating strikes into Cambodia and Laos seemed only a step away from calling for a full-scale invasion of northern Vietnam, and that appeared a political impossibility in terms of American domestic opinion, even in 1966. One thing was apparent in all of these discussions: for the men who thought in these terms Prince Sihanouk had become a bogy figure. His rotund physical appearance, his passionate, high-pitched speeches denouncing the United States, his public favouring of the Vietnamese Communist side, symbolised the basic cause for the frustrations that American planners felt about their role in Vietnam.

Nearly four years were to pass between the time when I heard this advocacy of an invasion of Cambodia and the time the invasion took place and I could not, in 1966, believe that such an event *would* take place. My estimation was wrong for I had failed to understand how obsessive the 'unpunished' Cambodian involvement in the Vietnam War could be to men who continued to believe that sooner or later the government in Hanoi would abandon its intentions of controlling all of Vietnam. Something deeper and more bitter than irony was involved in President Nixon's decision finally to commit American troops to an invasion of Cambodia in 1970 to achieve what he described as 'the most successful operation of this long and difficult war'. Richard Nixon had at last accepted the recommendations of his military and political planners. What they had been advocating for years with the aim of 'victory', he put into action. He did this, he said, to ensure American troops could continue withdrawing from southern Vietnam and so bring to an end an involvement that had poisoned United States domestic politics. Beyond the mockery of earlier military convictions there was the even more bitter consequence of the invasion. We cannot know what would have happened if the invasion had not taken place. What is beyond dispute is the assessment that the invasion was a major factor in advancing the Communist cause within Cambodia. The war had spread and cooperation between Cambodian and Vietnamese Communists became essential and productive. For a time the two groups of Communists had a common interest and they worked together to advance that interest in the 1970–75 period eventually to achieve the Communist victory over the Lon Nol forces in April 1975.

The last day I spent in Saigon in 1966 had nothing to do with Cambodia but in a minor fashion much to do with the dilemmas of human existence in a country at war. What I entered in my journal that night was this:

A bits and pieces day as I went about Saigon making my farewells. The archives staff, as had been the case for much of the time I spent working there, were engaged in some devious commercial transaction when I went to thank them. This is how it is, apparently, in so many of the government offices. But just what the archives staff is going to do with the hundreds of school exercise books, which seem to make up their latest commercial venture, is not clear to me. There must be a lack of exercise books—there must be to warrant hoarding hundreds of them in the way these men are doing. And when this lack becomes acute, presumably, they sell them at inflated prices. When costs such as the post office rates go up one hundred per cent, as they have just done, one must have some racket.

The chief librarian at the National Library was as depressed as ever. He has a brother in France, and undoubtedly the contrast between the untroubled life his brother leads and the difficulties of Saigon are just too real to be ignored.

And Pétrus Ky's grandson is leaving for France, another Vietnamese with French nationality who is getting out. When I went to say goodbye to him he was making his final plans to leave by ship in September. So often in Saigon one feels that one is witnessing human dramas—always tragedies, never comedies—which are being repeated over and over amongst the city's population. There are clearly other Vietnamese, such as Truong Vinh Tong, who are getting out while they can, but without any clear knowledge of what they are going to do once they get to France. There must be so many men like the little librarian who can see no path ahead but despair.

CHAPTER TWELVE

Business is Business

Trying to understand Cambodia's economy in 1966 was a little like looking at one of those mazes in a child's book where the entry and exit points are quite clear but the difficulty lies in how to get from one to the other. There was no problem in knowing the general state of Cambodia's economy and discussion of the dangerous, even disastrous position it had reached was part of the common coin of Phnom Penh conversation. But, like the maze in the child's puzzle book, arriving at the point of knowing just why matters were in such a parlous state presented countless difficulties. This was particularly so because despite the frequent discussion of the economy Cambodians talked about the matter with a shared background knowledge that was simply not available to a foreigner. It was only in the final weeks of my stay in Phnom Penh in 1966 that I heard, for instance, of Chou Kong.

I was riding in the car of a Sino–Cambodian friend in late August and as we made our way towards a small restaurant that lay a little distance from the city we passed a sizeable area of market gardens. These, my friend told me as if I would immediately grasp the significance of what he was saying, are also part of Chou Kong's operations. He was utterly surprised when I confessed that I had never heard of this man, and he proceeded to explain. Chou Kong was one of the most important, perhaps the most important, of the Chinese financiers in Cambodia. Little was known of his early life except that he had very humble origins and first worked as a coolie on the Phnom Penh waterfront.

112

Having succeeded in accumulating a little capital he then became an itinerant vendor. How he made the leap from such undistinguished employment to become an important figure in finance no one was certain, but in the 1950s he suddenly emerged into prominence through a number of commercial coups that firmly established his wealth. One feature of his rise to notable prosperity did seem beyond dispute. From the early 1950s Chou Kong had been in close touch with one of the most powerful of Sihanouk's elder advisers, Penn Nouth. The conviction was that, at very least, the association between these two men was of mutual benefit. It was the belief of the Phnom Penh business community that over the years Penn Nouth had been able to alert Chou Kong to prospective changes in various export and import regulations, or to planned changes in customs procedures and that this had allowed the businessman to make immense profits. Once those profits were made a percentage naturally went to Penn Nouth. Moreover, Chou Kong had further strengthened his position over the years by providing sympathetic assistance to political figures whose ambitions often outreached their financial resources.

Chou Kong's favourite business technique was classically simple and immensely profitable. He had, time and again, succeeded in cornering the market in various commodities. Only a few months before he had succeeded in buying up garlic, an essential component in Cambodian and Chinese cooking. When he released his stock he was assured of a profit of no less than five hundred per cent. Yet I had never heard of him.

The story of Chou Kong's rise to financial power and of his continuing success was, to carry the metaphor of the maze just a step further, one of those episodes along the way to understanding the Cambodian economy that had, like the alternative possibilities in a maze, to be assessed and explored before reaching the end of the puzzle, an end where the broad lines of the current situation were plain for all to see. These broad lines had, indeed, been fairly clear within a few weeks of my arrival in Phnom Penh, and barely a month had passed after that arrival when Sihanouk in one of his lengthy rambling speeches had stated bluntly, using a horseman's language, that the country's economy was 'blown'.

The economic situation of 1966 was linked directly to decisions that Sihanouk had taken in 1963. To the considerable surprise of most observers in Phnom Penh, and against the recommendations of his long-time adviser on economic matters, Son Sann, Sihanouk announced in November 1963 that he was introducing measures to nationalise the country's export and import trade, and that he was nationalising other industries and services including banks, insurance offices, and distilleries. He also announced his rejection of any further American aid. The reasons for his actions deserve attention. He argued that Cambodia should rely on its own resources and that in political terms the acceptance of American aid risked making Cambodia a client of the United States in the same dangerous fashion as had occurred in Laos and southern Vietnam. Moreover, he asserted that because of the extent to which the existing import and export business was in the hands of foreign nationals, most particularly Chinese and French businessmen, the country's political independence was further dangerously compromised.

What Sihanouk did not say in the public explanations of his decisions was that in acting as he did he was partially putting into practice ideas that had been advocated by young left-wing politicians, particularly Khieu Samphan and Hou Youn. Since in all probability he had been influenced by their arguments the irony of subsequent developments can scarcely be surpassed by any of the other many instances of irony that are such a feature of recent Cambodian history. Summarised and simplified the ironic progression is this: Inspired in part by the views of his leftist critics Sihanouk's austerity program of nationalisation and rejection of American aid was bitterly resented by the conservative elite upon whose support Sihanouk relied. As that elite saw their economic position eroding and grew more and more concerned about Cambodia's security position in relation to Vietnam a significant number of men on the right, with backing from the army, overthrew Sihanouk. This action, taken in March 1970, presaged Cambodia's full-scale involvement in the Second Indochinese War, Sihanouk's eventual total eclipse, and the final assumption of power by a Communist leadership of which Khieu Samphan was an important, if not dominant, figure.

Sihanouk's new economic policy introduced in 1963 was, beyond dispute, a factor in his subsequent fall. In 1966, however, as he continued to be the most important personality in Cambodian political life, it was he who gave repeated public testimony to the seriousness of the situation. What he was commenting on, when he deplored the run-down of the economy, was not just the economic ills of the country but its social and political problems as well. For one of the reasons why the reforms of 1963 did not fulfil the promise they initially showed was because of the prevailing pattern of corruption. And as he admitted with unconcealed chagrin, so far as corruption was concerned he had 'been beaten'.

Corruption touched every aspect of Cambodian life. The difference in 1966 was that corruption had increasingly ceased to be 'functional' and had, instead, become 'grand' in character. In the past, whether in the civilian or in the military ranks, widespread functional corruption was the normal state of affairs. Such corruption—the petty bribes, the pay-offs that ensured the award of contracts, the contributions that led to one person rather than another gaining a desired appointment—was the lubricant that kept the wheels of state moving. It may not have been admirable, but in general this type of corruption was kept within limits. In a country where few civil servants or military men could expect to live on their actual wages the system met a need. When Sihanouk introduced his new economic measures *and* cut off aid from the United States he created a new situation in which many of the sources of funds for functional corruption were removed. At the same time a whole range of other factors led the elite and the army to feel that their position was gravely threatened.

Foreign European businessmen may have decided that there was no profit to be made operating under the changed economic conditions, but the Chinese businessmen in Phnom Penh took a more positive view. Sihanouk had placed the state in charge of the import and export trade; clearly some accommodation would have to be found with the civil servants, particularly the most senior ones, who administered the system. In place of the system by which there had been a filtering of financial benefit from the highest ranks of the administration down through the lower echelons, the benefits now went to the wealthy and powerful who kept their gains to themselves. Evasions of the state system of import and export were legion and as men such as Chou Kong made their profits the state trading companies sank deeper and deeper into debt.

The elite were the more ready to grasp whatever major bribes they could with both hands since one of the results of Sihanouk's policies, and the subsequent breaking of diplomatic relations with the United States, was a sudden change in the Phnom Penh real estate market. For years the Cambodian elite had been investing in real estate that they let out at staggering rents to the foreign community. With the introduction of the new measures foreigners were no longer clamouring for houses and flats or ready to pay almost any price to get them. The American diplomatic mission was drastically reduced in size and then closed in 1964. The foreign personnel of the banks, the insurance offices, and the agency houses were no longer present to rival the diplomats in their capacity to meet the rental demands put to them. The American military aid mission had gone. In short, a major element in the real estate market, one that had played a vital part in forcing up rents to such inflated levels, abruptly disappeared.

Then there was the army. The conditions I had seen at Major Kim Kosal's camp in Kompong Chrey were duplicated all over Cambodia. From the point of view of national defence the rejection of American military aid appeared, in the eyes of many army officers, to be nothing short of disastrous. Quite apart from the provision of equipment by the United States to the Cambodian army, no less than thirty per cent of the entire armed forces budget was met from American funds in 1962, the last year before Sihanouk's rejection of further aid took place. One had to conclude that Sihanouk simply had not given any serious thought to the question of alternative financing for the armed forces. As financial difficulties grew greater army officers surveyed both the deteriorating military capacity of their units and of their own personal situation. No longer were there the possibilities for personal benefit that went with the American presence and the opportunity to attend courses at staff and command schools in the United States. If the army's role in Cambodia had continued to be essentially that of a disciplined civil aid group these circumstances might not have aroused quite such bitter resentment. In 1966, however, the army was increasingly being asked to carry out a true military role as it dealt with infiltration from Thailand and Vietnam and faced, in the latter case, the very real prospect of war spilling over the border. In these circumstances there was a striking conjunction of interests. For the Chinese businessmen in Phnom Penh with their family and clan links in the provinces, for the army officers who, away from the capital constituted the only real arm of government, and for the Vietnamese Communists there was a mutual interest in rice.

No one has pinpointed when the first significant clandestine shipments of rice started passing across the Cambodian-Vietnamese border to the shared benefit of the illegal traders and the recipients. So long as the conflict in Vietnam remained at a relatively low level the occasional smuggling of rice had no real significance for Cambodia. But the conflict in southern Vietnam continued to grow and did so at a time when the old patterns of commercial life in Cambodia had changed so that the state was now claiming the right to control all rice exports from the country. Rice was Cambodia's principal export crop, its major earner of foreign exchange. With a good rice harvest the government could look forward to the export earnings that sales abroad would earn. In addition it could count on the revenues produced by a system of internal duties, levied on the value of the exports before they left the country. This was the theory, but in 1966 the practice was very different.

As the war in Vietnam increasingly became a major conflict that pitched main force units of the contending sides against each other, so did the Communist forces have a growing demand for rice to feed their troops. For rice to reach them from Cambodia all manner of laws and regulations had to be breached, but the obstacles were so efficiently overcome that during 1966 somewhere between a third and a half of the entire Cambodian rice harvest was sold illegally to the Communists in Vietnam. What took place was a massive, even national conspiracy to defeat the regulations laid down by Sihanouk's government in Phnom Penh. The laws said that the farmers should sell their surplus crop to the government, but the government did not pay in cash at the time of the sale and the price it offered was less than that offered by the Chinese merchants. Moreover, for all the rules and regulations to the contrary, the Chinese merchants in the countryside were still very much a part of the rice farmers' world. They were still ready to provide seed and fertilizer on credit in the way that the government agencies either could not or would not do. Once the rice was in the hands of the merchants they had no hesitation in breaking the laws against illegal export, for as ethnic Chinese or Sino–Cambodians who had been settled in the country for seldom more than two generations, they still held fast to the view that the only laws that mattered were those of their own family or clan. The law of the Cambodians, as with the law of the French colonial power before, was ignored when it could be, or circumvented when it could not be disregarded.

Since verifiable statistics will never be available it is impossible to know the exact level of profits that were made by these merchants. That profits were enormous is testified to by a whole range of indicators. The size of the illegal trade in smuggled rice alone tells its own story. The fact that in excess of one third of the country's export crop was siphoned off illegally in 1966 emphasises how attractive this commerce was. Again, the generally agreed price that had to be paid by the merchants to the military men who permitted or prevented trucks carrying rice to pass through their districts was an accurate reflection of a high rate of profit. For a merchant to be able to pay fifteen hundred American dollars for each truck of rice that drove to the border, or just beyond, argues for a very substantial return. Without anyone being sure of just how much rice was crossing the border in 1966 there seemed to be general agreement in Phnom Penh that the amount was on the increase, and that in the border regions the Chinese trading and commercial community prospered in stark contrast to the economic decline in so much of the rest of the country. Indeed, I saw one striking if minor illustration of this myself.

The market town of Tonleap lies almost on the border between Cambodia and Vietnam. In June I had travelled south into Takeo province to visit Major Kim Kosal. I made a mistake and went beyond my intended destination of Kompong Chrey to Tonleap. Sited not far from some low, scrub covered hills, Tonleap had an unprepossessing appearance. The wet season had already begun in June, but on the morning I reached Tonleap the sun was shining through a light haze and had been sufficiently hot to dry out the ground so that the gusting wind was blowing clouds of fine dust off the unpaved streets. There was not much to the town; a central market, some shophouses, a few eating houses, all in need of paint, and all Chinese. Even if I had not expected the population of Tonleap to be overwhelmingly Chinese it would not have taken me long to learn that this was so. At the back of each shop or eating house the walls were covered with pictures of the Chinese leadership. In the eating house to which I retreated for a glass of beer the display of pictures covered many square feet and was distinguished less by the enormous coloured portrait of Mao Tse-tung as by the most unattractive picture that I had ever seen of Chen Yi, the Chinese Foreign Minister. This display of Nanyang Chinese pride in his or his parents' homeland seemed the only part of the shop that had received the least care. The furniture was ramshackle, the walls almost as discoloured with dirt as the floor, and the beer was warm.

Only three months later this eating house was transformed. In September I journeyed south to Tonleap once again, this time to climb the nearby hill on which sits the Bayang ruin, a temple dating from before the foundation of the ancient Angkorian empire at the beginning of the ninth century. It had looked an easy climb from the road but like so much in the Cambodian countryside this was deceptive. For about three quarters of the way there was a path to follow, though it was steeper than I would have guessed when looking from below. Then, for the last section, a barely defined track wound through thick secondary growth until, at the very end, one climbed to the sanctuary over the laterite steps laid down more than a thousand years before. Having climbed and descended this six hundred foot hill even the lukewarm beer of a Tonleap eating house seemed immensely inviting. But that was not what I had to consume. Returning to the same shop I had patronised in June I found that the beer was iced. It was brought to me in a frosted bottle from a large, brand-new refrigerator. The ramshackle furniture had become new chrome and plastic chairs. The walls had been painted, and even the floor seemed cleaner. What had not changed, apart from the presence of the same dour-looking owner, was the pictorial display. Pinned against the now freshly

painted wall was the same gallery symbolising Peking's power and
place at the centre of this overseas Chinese merchant's universe.
And still dominating the group, eclipsing Mao and Chou En-lai
was the striking picture of an apparently malevolent Chen Yi.

I did not need to consult statistics to know what had happened
for this man and for others. Just what part they played in the
rice smuggling trade I do not know. They might merely have aided
in the transfer of the rice sacks from the trucks to the sampans
that at this time of the year could come almost to the backdoors
of the shops and move across the flooded paddy fields that lay
between Cambodia and Vietnam. Or perhaps, despite his appearance, the man who ran the eating house was a person of
considerable wealth with a major interest in the illegal rice trade.
Appearance was never any guide to the possession of wealth among
these country merchants. That he had benefited was clear. This
Chinese merchant, army officers, and in their own small way the
farmers who had sold their rice illegally in the first place all
benefited. None of this could have taken place if there had not
been influential men and women in the capital who were ready
to ensure that the trade went on and that they gained from it.
Sihanouk hinted at the role played by the wives of high officials.
Gossips spoke of how senior members of the royal family were
implicated. These people thrived mightily in 1966 as a poor harvest
earlier in the year led to shortages both in Cambodia and Vietnam,
and with the shortages came a rapid rise in price.

Rice was the major commodity passing across the border illegally
in 1966. A limited number of weapons may have been shipped
across the border in that year but not until the end of the sixties
did the clandestine passage of arms become significant. Quantities
of medical supplies, however, were often passed across the border.
Payment of a major bribe would give a Phnom Penh businessman
access to foreign exchange and so to the international market. But
the drugs and pharmaceutical supplies he subsequently bought
never appeared on the domestic market. There was a particular
attraction to this commodity since the profit on a single truckload
of medical supplies was much greater than the profit on rice. As
might be expected, the price paid to the army officer who permitted

a truckload of medical supplies to pass through his territory was many times higher than the price he received for those trucks loaded with grain.

There seemed no way to stop the rot. Even those few able Cambodian officials who struggled to implement the broad lines of Sihanouk's 1963 decisions found they could not contend with the Prince's sudden and unpredictable forays into the economic field. One of these men was Cheam Vann, the head of SONEXIM (the National Company for Exports and Importers). It seems unlikely that he was totally outside the system of corruption that flourished in 1966, but there seemed to be general agreement that he was by the standards of the time a notably honest man. He was also efficient and possessed formal economic training. As the head of SONEXIM he had been responsible for that body's initial success before it found its position undermined by the growing illegal trading. He was a man of independent judgment and had, in the immediate post-Second World War period, been associated with Prince Sisowath Youtevong in opposition to those politicians who were ready to accord major political power to the then young King Sihanouk. Such a past record was something that Sihanouk could never completely forgive even if he might temporarily appear to forget the facts of the past.

In April 1966 Sihanouk was well aware that his economic measures were not working. Acting once again without seeking advice Sihanouk summoned Cheam Vann and ordered him to expand SONEXIM's operations to include the purchasing of all agricultural products produced within Cambodia as well as the control of their sales abroad. Cheam Vann protested that this was an undertaking SONEXIM simply could not handle. Its capacities were already stretched and he had neither the staff nor the organisation to do what Sihanouk asked. As Cheam Vann continued to oppose this proposed new measure Sihanouk became furious. When he toured Svay Rieng and Prey Veng provinces in early May he regaled his peasant audiences with long diatribes on the iniquities of Phnom Penh society and accounts of the difficulties he faced because of the self-interested and obstructive civil servants with whom he had to deal. Cheam Vann's name figured prominently in the denunciations. Stung by such public criticism Cheam Vann resigned.

Such a resignation by a very senior official with a high reputation could not be overlooked. The semi-official newspaper, *Réalités Cambodgiennes*, felt it necessary in its 20 May issue to argue that the criticisms Sihanouk had made of certain officials were 'without doubt severe, but certainly not offensive'. This was not how capital gossip spoke of the affair. Tired and dispirited as he was Sihanouk was said to have, even more than usual, resorted to gutter invective in his provincial speeches, on one occasion referring to Cheam Vann as a 'dog', a particularly offensive term of Cambodian abuse. Among Sihanouk's older advisers the departure of Cheam Vann at this time of continuing economic decline seemed likely to add yet another factor making for uncertainty and concern. So convinced were they of Cheam Vann's ability that they were prepared to take the unusual step of seeking to have Sihanouk change his mind. Following his return from the provinces Sihanouk had announced that he was cancelling a planned trip to France for medical treatment and was going to go into hospital in Phnom Penh instead. It was General Nhiek Tioulong, the Inspector General of the army, recent 'star' in 'Apsara' and one of Sihanouk's oldest colleagues who braved the Prince's displeasure as he lay in his bed at the Fondation Calmette hospital. Tioulong suggested to Sihanouk that it would be in the general interest for Cheam Vann to remain as head of SONEXIM. Sihanouk flew into a terrible rage, his wrath driving the general from the room. When Cheam Vann did return to public life it was in the final phases of the Sihanouk years, the period from early 1968 onwards when the right began to show itself ready to act without direction from the Prince or even against his wishes. Given his experience in 1966 there was no surprise in this later period to find Cheam Vann's name associated with the growing conservative opposition to Sihanouk's capricious rule.

There were times when it was hard to take the complaints of the Phnom Penh elite very seriously as they deplored their declining personal economic position. For someone dependent on a graduate student's stipend the complaint of a friend that he now had to make do with Red Label rather than Black Label Johnny Walker whisky was scarcely a cause for excessive sympathy. Yet this man like many others felt he was being hurt by the decline taking place. More slowly than some, but being hurt nonetheless. Increasingly he was drawing on capital to maintain the standard of living he had come to expect in the boom years of the late fifties and the early sixties. Several of the houses that he had previously let out to foreigners were empty. Like so many of his fellows the state of the economy dominated his thinking, and in Sihanouk's Cambodia it was only to be expected that the Prince should become the object for blame. The growing tide of criticism was founded on solid traditional grounds as well as on the facts of the present. In Cambodian history it was clear that a ruler could be forgiven many things if he assured the well-being of his officials. Failure to do so placed a king's position at risk. Sihanouk's policies placed him at risk in terms of the right's conviction that in serving his interests he no longer served theirs.

The interests of the conservative elite were not hard to perceive and their reaction to the continuing slide in the economy were predictable. Less easy to assess was the reaction of the left. If they welcomed the general thrust of Sihanouk's policies they could only deplore the actual results these had generated. For those men and women who were undecided about the desirability of a left-wing solution to Cambodia's ills, the rampant corruption and the unrestrained venality that was apparent for all to see in 1966 must have gone a long way towards convincing them that no compromise was possible. Once again stress needed to be given, so far as the left-wing was concerned, to the offensiveness of the system over which Sihanouk presided. I suspect I saw an example of this less than two weeks before I left Cambodia in September 1966. A fellow guest at a drinks party one evening was Prince Sisowath Dusadey, one of Sisowath Entaravong's children. I knew him as little more than a passing acquaintance and my image of him was of a young man readily classified as a playboy. As an apparently typical young man about town he had been married to Nhiek Tioulong's daughter before her flagrant infidelities brought an end to the marriage. Regarded as an accomplished dancer, he was recruited by Sihanouk to be one of the extras in a scene in his film showing a party in progress. In short, Dusadey seemed yet another self-indulgent and therefore unremarkable young Cambodian prince.

That he was something more than this was soon apparent when I found myself talking with him. As in so many other chance conversations during that year it was the economy that was discussed. Dusadey worked in the offices of the Magasin d'Etat, the state enterprise responsible for distributing consumer goods to retailers throughout the country. He was not happy in his job. First there were the Prince's unjustified criticisms of the Magasin's staff. Sihanouk, it appeared, had become dissatisfied with the nature of the goods that the Magasin was handling. Earlier in the year he had criticised the head of the Magasin for stocking so much imported processed milk. How could one respond to criticism of this sort, Dusadey asked? There was a demand for milk which the health services had encouraged mothers and children to drink and, apart from the insanitary operations of a few Pakistanis who kept a small herd of diseased-looking cows on the outskirts of the capital, Cambodia produced no milk. The whole thing was typical of Sihanouk's policies. He was ready to make sweeping decisions at a moment's notice, but he seldom thought through the longer-term implications. That, however, was only part of the problem. Placed as he was in the Magasin d'Etat, Dusadey was in a position to judge just how greedy the Cambodian business community actually was. In a way it was puzzling that he should have been so surprised. Yet there was no doubt that he was; he was surprised and offended. The businessmen, he went on angrily, were not satisfied unless they could make one hundred and fifty per cent profit. For them to think in terms of a reasonable ten per cent was derisory. Was Sisowath Dusadey giving me some clue to his inner political convictions in this casual exchange? At the time I did not make such a judgment. Later I had cause to think again for following Sihanouk's overthrow Sisowath Dusadey was one of the men who chose to join the insurgents in the countryside. By any standards that choice was a major and a dangerous one. I can only guess at the extent to which his experiences in 1966 contributed to it.

The economic decline that was so apparent in 1966 had acted like a catalyst to speed the political process towards some resolution of Cambodia's many problems, even if that resolution was only a temporary one. Sihanouk's economic decisions taken three years before, the developing war in Vietnam, the poor rice crop harvested at the beginning of the year were interacting factors which affected a far wider range of the population than had been the case before. Compared to the economic situation some six or seven years before, the conditions in 1966 provided a sharp and disturbing contrast. In principle Sihanouk's determination expressed in his 1963 decisions to follow economic policies that assured Cambodia's independence was admirable. But his new policies were introduced in circumstances that gave little weight to principle and much to expedience. The problem of widespread corruption that flourished as Sihanouk pursued his programme of austerity belied the picture the Prince had so often proclaimed of the Cambodian state united in common purpose. When to this basic lack of unity was added the accelerating conflict in Vietnam, something over which Sihanouk had no control, he was faced with a threat and a problem that he could not meet without some basic change in strategy.

The decision to make such a change seems to have been taken in July 1966, though its subsequent implementation was piecemeal. Nothing could disguise the difficulties the country faced in economic terms, and there were insistent voices in his own entourage who begged him to reconsider his policy of friendship for the Vietnamese Communists. From July 1966 onwards Sihanouk took a number of decisions that showed he had concluded his and Cambodia's salvation lay with the ascendancy of the right. To begin with he had responded warmly to the suggestion that Averell Harriman should visit Cambodia to discuss possible resumption of diplomatic relations between Cambodia and the United States. The fact that this invitation was later withdrawn as the result of the Thlok Trach border incidents did not, in the long run, affect the general drift of a policy that eventually led to the resumption of diplomatic ties and to Sihanouk giving his clandestine agreement to President Nixon's plan to carry out secret bombing strikes against Vietnamese Communist forces in Cambodia.

As far as internal policies were concerned, Sihanouk appears never to have fully understood how bitterly his austerity programmes were resented by the armed forces. This was curious since he had no illusions concerning the right-wing political inclinations of the officer corps. One has to suppose that he was genuine in believing that gestures such as dedicating the film 'Apsara' to the officers and men of the armed forces were able to outweigh the factors that caused such discontent, particularly in the army. But he was alert to the shifts in the overt political world and to the fact of deepening elite discontent. This awareness led him to take two fateful decisions. The first was taken in August 1966 when he announced he would not involve himself in selecting the candidates who would stand for election to Cambodia's parliament the following month. This decision, which contrasted with Sihanouk's actions in previous elections, had a clear and widely understood significance. With Sihanouk no longer personally involved in selecting candidates the field was thrown open for the most blatant vote-buying, and the men who had the money to buy votes were the right-wing politicians. The second fateful decision followed upon the first. When, as expected, the right triumphed in the September 1966 elections Sihanouk approved the National Assembly's nomination of General Lon Nol to be the new prime minister. In doing so Sihanouk set his former close associate on the path that led inexorably to the Prince's ignominious deposition in March 1970.

CHAPTER THIRTEEN

Another Cambodia

Less than half an hour's drive from Phnom Penh was the small town of Kompong Kantuot, an unremarkable but attractive settlement with a basically Chinese population living in the 'standard' shophouses along a main street running parallel with the Prek Thnot River. I knew a little about Kompong Kantuot's history from a document I had seen in the archives. Its existence as a small market town dated from the early twentieth century. Before that there had been a small Cambodian village there, but as fifty years of a French colonial presence had their effect and a measure of calm became the norm rather than the exception in the countryside Kompong Kantuot's strategic position on a river marked it out for growth as a minor commercial centre. Cambodian farmers had been ready to sell land to Chinese immigrants who recognised the opportunities opening up before them. Without the disorder that had been so constant a part of Cambodia's history for hundreds of years it became possible for farmers to grow more rice than was necessary simply for their own needs. With a surplus of rice there was an opportunity for a rice merchant. As well there were opportunities for merchants who sold tools, household goods and cloth. The first decade of the twentieth century saw a minor economic boom in Cambodia and in 1903, a French official reported, one way that this was reflected in Kompong Kantuot was in the presence of no less than three tailors. Even that number could barely keep up with the volume of business that a sudden new prosperity had generated.

But if I knew something of Kompong Kantuot's history I knew

nothing of the village that lay a further ten minute's drive beyond the town. This was the 'model village' of Anlong Romiet and one morning in late April 1966 I found myself travelling there with no less a companion that I.F. Stone, the remarkable Washington journalist whose famous weekly newsletter reflected its author's deep distrust of government and his infinite capacity to pierce through a politician's or civil servant's protective shields of cant, secrecy, and hypocrisy. I.F. Stone was making his first visit to Cambodia and the Ministry of Information had arranged for him to visit Anlong Romiet so that he could see what life in the countryside was like. He suggested I should accompany him so as to translate from French into English, and I gladly did.

At first glance the model village did not seem very different from hundreds of other villages that I had seen. Houses set on piles were scattered irregularly over a couple of acres of ground with fruit trees and sugar palms growing in profusion near to the edges of the settlement. There was a central well, which was not unusual, but certainly not universal. The longer I looked at the village, however, the more I began to sense what gave it a 'model' character. There was a singular lack of animals, no scavenging pigs, no mangey dogs cringing at the expectation of a kick but hoping for a scrap of food. If this was a model village it was also an unreal village and a tour of two or three of the houses added confirmation to this estimate. We were shown houses containing heavy overpadded arm chairs and, even more amazing, European-style beds covered with candlewick bedspreads. But it was our guide who brought home to me the most striking unreality of all as he went on and on about the feature of the village that he clearly saw as being of the utmost importance. Each house, the man from the ministry proudly repeated, each house had its own *cabinet*. Indeed, each house did have its own lavatory and as this was pointed out I realised what was really missing from this village and what set it apart from the real villages of Cambodia. It lacked the all-pervasive, slightly sweet and sharp smelling odour of human shit that was so characteristic of Cambodian villages with their primitive sanitation.

Villages were not a part of Cambodia I knew well. It was not that I had never visited them for I had done so dozens, probably hundreds, of times. But they were a world I could not penetrate.

My Southeast Asian language was Vietnamese, not Cambodian and outside the ranks of the elite the use of French was very limited. Yet it was from the countryside that the leaders of Cambodia's revolution drew their most important support. It was the country boys and girls who became the dedicated soldiers who were finally able to defeat a much better armed and equipped body of troops after sustaining years of the most intense aerial bombardment ever directed against any target. Was there anything in what I knew of the Cambodian countryside, of its villages and the farmers who lived in them that hinted at the future?

It is hard to be sure. Or, perhaps more accurately, it is all too easy to look back and to project on to the memories of 1966 information culled subsequently from the small amount of research that has been devoted to Cambodian rural life in an effort to find an explanation for the success of Cambodia's rural-based revolution. Even if one succumbs to this temptation the plain fact of the matter is that the amount of serious examination scholars give to life in rural Cambodia is limited indeed. There is a real problem about making generalisations since one of the points that does seem clear is the extent to which conditions in one area often differed very considerably from those in another. And if one moves away from the recorded results of research by economists and human geographers how much reliance can be placed on the impressions formed by a traveller unable to break the barrier of language? I can write of what I saw, and in doing so draw up impressions gained in the course of widespread travel in Cambodia during the nearly three and a half years I lived there over a period of twelve years. But no one is more conscious than I am of the fact that my impressions will not answer the questions that are being debated among the small group of scholars and government servants in the West who continue to take an interest in Cambodia. There are, I think, two key questions so far as the Cambodian countryside is concerned. The first relates to the 'why' of the Cambodian revolution. Was it the case that conditions in the rural areas were so bad that once a rebellion broke out against the government in one area this was sufficient to spark peasant reaction throughout the country as a whole? The second concerns the 'how' of the revolution. How did a city-based leadership of men who were, in Cambodian terms, very much intellectuals, succeed in gaining the support of important sections of the rural population and manage to fire them with the passion and belief to fight against terrifying odds to achieve their political goals? As I think of the problems of penetrating to the reality of rural Cambodia—another Cambodia from that of the capital I knew so well—I wonder if satisfactory answers will ever be found.

There was much that was deceptive about the Cambodian countryside. By the middle of the rainy season and for some two months after the rains had ceased the omnipresent green of vegetation and foliage gave a false impression of abundant water and lush fecundity. In fact, Cambodia was a country where water was in short supply. Crops could grow and thrive where water was readily available but away from the rivers and with only a limited amount of artificial irrigation vast areas of land were unproductive. Almost every basic guide to Cambodia noted the sparseness of human settlement. Considerably less than half of the theoretically arable land of the country was cultivated. For very good reasons. Much of the land that was not farmed was not irrigated and without irrigation the risk of crop failure hung like a recurrent but unpredictable phantom before any cultivator who was foolhardy enough to ignore the uncertainty of the monsoon rains. No exaggeration is involved in the simple but always potentially devastating fact that should the rains not come in their normal fashion a Cambodian peasant farmer could face not just want but famine.

Deception was present in other ways. Once I had come to observe the people of the countryside with a little more care and perception I became aware of an apparently curious feature. There always seemed a considerable number of young people in the countryside, ranging from the apparently carefree children to young men and women in their late teens or, perhaps, early twenties. But then there appeared to be a demographic gap with little evidence of people whom one might judge to be in their thirties or forties. After the young there were the old men and women, their faces creased by the sun, toothless or nearly so, their frames bent from work in the rice fields. The deception here lay in the fact that these *were* the men and women in their thirties and forties. Men and women became old in appearance so much earlier than an observer from the West expected. The harsh conditions of labour and living ensured that this would be so. The demands of work in the rice fields were much greater than many an outsider realised; it was back-breaking and repetitive labour carried out under a burning sun. Of course there were men who lived into their sixties and longer. But so often the peasant man or woman whom I judged to be already of an advanced age was only some forty years old. The harsh reality of Cambodian rural life was told in the statistics for life expectancy. In the 1960s the life expectancy for both men and women did not extend beyond forty-five.

The demanding work in the fields was not the only reason for this prospect of what, in Western terms, was an early death. Endemic disease was another, indeed the other major reason for the relatively brief lives or utter wretchedness of so many of the rural population. In some rural areas malaria had been brought under control. But in other regions the disease remained entrenched so that virtually the entire population suffered to one degree or another. Dysentery was a constant and debilitating fact of life over wide areas, as were such other scourges as trachoma, yaws, tuberculosis, and venereal disease. The picture of a happy contented peasantry that some foreign observers took away with them after a brief visit to Cambodia was false. What was more startling was that this false image was believed by some of the Cambodian elite who allowed themselves to be convinced that there was no cause for concern about conditions in the rural areas. Indeed Sihanouk himself was not immune to the error of accepting this false picture. Even after his deposition he would speak wistfully of the supposedly happy life led by the peasants in the days before his fall, still believing that the people had actually enjoyed the benefits of life in something approaching an earthly paradise.

The statistics for death and disease are fairly clearly established. Less clearly defined are other statistics that might tell us more about the discontent present in the countryside. Some basic facts of rural Cambodian life are apparently beyond dispute, though even with these there may be need for qualification. The countryside was not, in contrast for instance to southern Vietnam, marked by the harsh predominance of landlordism, a situation in which property is owned by a few wealthy men and worked by tenant farmers, or even worse, in terms of social and economic disadvantage, by landless labourers. With some important exceptions, such as areas in Battambang province, the farmers of Cambodia worked their own land. The exception of Battambang was important, since this was the province in which the Samlaut Rebellion broke out in 1967; the rural revolt that signalled the start of significant armed struggle in the countryside. What is difficult to gauge is whether the absence of landlordism meant that there were no other major socio–economic rural problems. Statistics are either incomplete or unreliable so that no entirely satisfactory conclusions can be reached. A few facts seem beyond dispute. It is quite certain that the problem of indebtedness was widespread. And with indebtedness went usury. The problem is to know the scale of the debts involved and the interest charged. Figures on this question are incomplete or in dispute for Cambodia as a whole, and the reality of what the figures on debt meant is difficult, even impossible to assess. Once again I have to turn back to the impressionistic picture. For the few who thought and talked about this matter in Cambodia's capital in 1966 there seemed to be a widespread acceptance that usury was a dominant fact in the lives of a great many of the rural population. Rice merchants, who were usually ethnic Chinese or Sino–Cambodians, held many of the peasant farmers in a grip that tightened every year. Government efforts to break the hold of the merchants had achieved limited success.

When the harsh facts of Cambodian rural life are reviewed, however, there can be no doubt that whatever problems and deprivations existed these were not of an order comparable to what existed in pre-1949 China or to what still exists in parts of contemporary India or Bangladesh. Moreover, it may be that we know too little about the conditions endured by those who lived on the fringe of rural society. I had a sense of there being such fringe regions when, in the course of a visit to Pursat, a town mid-way between Phnom Penh and Battambang, I made enquiries about the 'marble' quarries that lay to the west in the foothills of the Cardamom mountains. The product of these quarries was not true marble but a soapstone in a range of colours that was worked into small decorative items in Pursat. There seemed something romantic in what I had heard of blocks of the stone being brought out of the distant ranges by elephants before being transferred to ox carts for the slow journey to Pursat. The romance I had conjured up was quickly dispelled when I talked with an official in the local administration at Pursat. He seemed to regard the workers in the quarries as little more than savages. Certainly he would never risk his health by travelling to sites from which the stone was extracted. They were located in malarial regions and the quarry workers universally suffered from this disease. Why, I asked, still capable of remarkable innocence, did the workers remain there, enduring harsh labour that brought them little return and constantly expose themselves and their families to a crippling disease? The response was offered in some surprise: But what else could they do?

The reply was one I thought about then and have wondered about since. If the conditions of rural life were not as dreadful in Cambodia in the mid-1960s as they have been and are elsewhere what did this really tell an observer about how an individual Cambodian saw his or her lot? The quarry workers west of Pursat were a special case, just as the various hill peoples of eastern Cambodia were occupiers of a very different fringe location. But the official in Pursat had made one thing very clear. Opportunity to move from one place in society to another was not something that a rural Cambodian could assume existed. How could a quarryman break out of that cycle of existence? He could not easily, if ever, transform himself into a farmer, even though Cambodian custom vested land ownership in the hands of the man who tilled the ground. To become a farmer one needed capital for seed, for tools, and for fertilizer. An occasional member of the quarryman's fringe group might make the transition, but this would be the rarest exception that proved the rule.

Were the frustrations associated with a rural existence that provided so little opportunity for breaking out of time-ordained patterns of existence part of the deeper explanation for the drift of so many young Cambodians to Phnom Penh? The lure of the capital was not to be discounted. It promised a life far removed from that of the rural villages. The promise for most, however, went unfulfilled. And yet the young men and women having made the break chose to stay in the city. They stayed and performed the most menial jobs rather than return to their country homes. For the young men the docks or employment as a pedicab—the *cyclopousse* in local terminology—rider were the obvious options. I have never tried to carry the heavy loads that were manhandled by the dockers along Phnom Penh's waterfront, but I have tried the experience of pedalling a *cyclopousse*. One has to imagine propelling and manoeuvring a three-wheeled vehicle several times heavier than an ordinary bicycle, to which the further weight of one, two, or even three persons has been added. As a game at a party the physical effort is a passing joke. But life for the *cyclopousse* men was far from that. They lived on the margin of existence. Renting their vehicle from a Chinese entrepeneur they had to struggle every day in order to take sufficient money in fares to first pay the rental and then to pay for their food. There was no question which must come first. Failure to pay the daily rental meant the end of employment. They rode their pedicabs in every kind of weather, wringing wet with rain in the wet season and soaked with sweat in the dry. Tuberculosis was the trade's distinctive disease and an early death was the sombre expectation. But there were always other young newcomers ready to take the place of those who died or finally admitted they could ride no more; new young men for whom the costs of existence in Phnom Penh for some reason outweighed the costs they saw of existence in the countryside.

In the final analysis we may never know just what it was that enabled the Cambodian Communist leaders to gain the support they did. Was life in the villages so dreadful that men and women were ready to embrace the ultimate risk of death to achieve change? Of course coercion played its part, but any attempt to understand rural revolution in Cambodia that does not look beyond coercion would be dishonest and misleading. I am forced to conclude that in 1966 I could see but I could not understand the deeper realities of rural Cambodia. I could see the scattered villages gathered near their sugar palm trees in a landscape that seemed infinite under the washed-out sky of the late dry season. At that time of the year dust obscured distant features or rose like a smoke pall as a convoy of ox carts ploughed along an unsurfaced road. I could see the countryside transformed by the rains, with the bright green of the rice fields, and the darker green of the other vegetation and foliage sluiced clean by the storms of the monsoon. But I could understand only the most basic and possibly the least important aspects of what I saw. Passing through the small settlements strung out along the main highways I could tell that commerce was in the hands of immigrants, or the descendants of immigrants, and that the rice mill was seldom if ever owned by a Cambodian. Once again, just what this all meant beyond the obvious was unknown to me.

I had studied Cambodian peasant involvement in rebellions and protest movements in historical times, in the nineteenth and early twentieth centuries. One conclusion did seem to emerge from an effort to explain why many thousands of peasant Cambodians were ready to rise up and revolt against established authority in those earlier periods. The conclusion was that peasant dissent was in itself real, and that it was most likely to occur in periods of basic instability. Was there such basic instability in Cambodian rural life in 1966? The answer for parts of Battambang province may be firm and affirmative. For other areas the case is less clear so that mystery about aspects of fact and motive may always be a part of attempts to understand this other, rural Cambodia.

CHAPTER FOURTEEN

Scribes and Sycophants

While he still dominated Cambodian politics Prince Norodom Sihanouk was a mimic's delight. He has a distinctive, high-pitched yet readily imitated voice. When he speaks French, as he does frequently in speeches and at news conferences, his delivery is punctuated by nervous laughter and marked by much repetition. At times of emotion his voice rises higher and higher and the nervous laughter seems as if it risks dominating the words as the Prince struggles to keep himself under control. Few foreigners resident in Phnom Penh could resist an occasional imitation of Sihanouk in full verbal flood, but there was one man who could offer a virtuoso performance and successfully mimic every characteristic of a princely speech. It would all be there; the spate of words increasingly interrupted by near-hysterical laughter, the rising pitch of the already high voice, each and every inflection. And because it was mimicry it was also mockery. Such a performance in the sensitive atmosphere of Phnom Penh came close to *lèse-majesté*, and it was usually reserved for private parties at which no Cambodians were present. But occasionally the man in question might be seen and heard, surrounded by cronies quietly performing his mimicry in one of the French-style cafés that still managed to operate in 1966. Indeed, it was in one of these, shortly after I arrived in Phnom Penh that year, that I first heard this strikingly successful imitation.

What was interesting about the performances was not merely their notable success in imitating Sihanouk. Equally interesting was the fact that the man who gave them was one of Sihanouk's

French 'experts', in this case a man who worked as a *speaker* at the Cambodian radio service and who, with one or two others of his countrymen, gave the French language programmes that unmistakable French character marked by extremely fast speech and all kinds of 'voice-over' techniques combining simultaneous talk and music. But more than that, the man who imitated Sihanouk so well was also in considerable demand as the mellifluous voiced master of ceremonies at such events as the world premier of 'Apsara' to sing the praises of the Prince and Cambodia. Perhaps I should not have been surprised to find that a man whose private view of Sihanouk was mockingly dismissive should, in public, be the regime's spokesman. Nevertheless I was surprised and continued to be so as I found that one after another of the Frenchmen who worked for Sihanouk as journalists, speechwriters, and general advisers, were highly critical of the Prince himself and cared little if anything for the country in which they worked. Loyalty to Sihanouk was perhaps more than should have been expected, but discretion had seemed likely. Neither operated in Sihanouk's Cambodia in 1966.

I simply do not know how many foreigners worked in the Prince's employ. Undoubtedly the number varied from period to period, and overall there may not have been more than a dozen directly employed in Sihanouk's service. The number of Frenchmen working in various other capacities in the Cambodian administration was much higher. Small though their numbers were their presence was important, just how important is still a matter for dispute. At a practical level it was they who ensured the production of much of the press and magazine material published by the Cambodian government. The weekly semi-official news-paper, *Réalités Cambodgiennes*, was edited by a Frenchman. Frenchmen worked as Sihanouk's employees to produce *Kambuja* and the *Sangkum*, two magazines Sihanouk established in the early sixties during his period of enthusiasm for journalism. French speechwriters wrote for Sihanouk and upon instructions produced summarised and bowdlerised French versions of his lengthy, often rambling, and frequently earthy Cambodian speeches. It was also they who wrote the accounts of the Prince's daily doings. This was not in the form of a 'court circular' with a brief statement of Sihanouk's activities. Instead these *plumatifs*, these scribblers —some Cambodians were more blunt and called them mercenaries —produced panegyrics that invested every princely action with immense import. In 1966 the specialist in these matters was a Monsieur Fuchs who was master of a prose style that trembled with adulation and echoed the baroque character of another age, that of Louis XIV.

Whether Fuchs was happy in his job I do not know. There were others, such as Loïc Evan, who were not. He had come to Cambodia from Paris knowing little of the country or its politics but thinking that the experience of working in close proximity to Prince Sihanouk would be interesting. When writing for the *Sangkum* and *Kambuja*, he found that he was expected to produce copy in which no praise for Sihanouk could be excessive and no hint of a critical observation concerning the country would be tolerated. He was also drawn into the business of answering the fulsome letters that Sihanouk received from his admirers around the world. This was one of the curious aspects of Cambodian affairs. Throughout his governance of Cambodia Sihanouk attracted a stream of letters from admirers and well wishers. The bulk of these appeared to come from France and many were written in such excessively adulatory terms that one was tempted to see some of them as jokes. Perhaps this was wrong and the affirmations of devotion despatched from obscure provincial addresses were entirely genuine and neither a joke nor, as some cynically suggested, sent in the sole interest of gaining in return a letter on princely notepaper signed by Sihanouk's own hand. In any event, the letters had to be answered, and the illusion preserved that Sihanouk drafted all the replies himself.

In this atmosphere of constant sycophancy two figures stood out among the cringe of courtiers. The first, and by far the better known among those who had some experience of Cambodia, was Charles Meyer. The other, and editor of *Réalités Cambodgiennes,* was Jean Barré. Rather surprisingly I had not met Charles Meyer during my first extended stay in Cambodia in 1959–61. His name, and his various reputations, were well-known to me but not the man himself. He was a person of some mystery. Since he never talked about his pre-Cambodian past in my presence the picture I have constructed of his background comes from many sources, some certainly less reliable than others. He is a Frenchman, from Alsace. Dennis Bloodworth, the noted British journalist who knew him in Vietnam, suggests that Meyer as a younger man looked like Molotov's son with his round glasses and squarish face. A different and more general comparison came to my mind when I first saw him in 1966. With his nondescript hair, glasses, and stern face he looked like a model for a French provincial school teacher. There was something about the intensity of his gaze, coupled with an air of being hardly done by, of not having his talents sufficiently appreciated, that smacked of the pedantic, professionally unsuccessful teacher who felt his capacities were being wasted in the provinces.

Meyer had come to Phnom Penh from Saigon, where his role in the political manoeuvring that accompanied the closing stages of the First Indochina War and the rise to power of Ngo Dinh Diem remains obscure. He is said to have been trained as a geographer, and there is no doubting his cartographic abilities. But he quite certainly was something more. Whatever meaning one attaches to the term, he was an 'adviser' to Bay Vien, the leader of the Saigon-based quasi-military group called the Binh Xuyen. This group had run the major Saigon rackets after 1946, drawing immense profits from gambling and prostitution. But more than this they controlled the Saigon police and the city's internal security service. As France painfully conceded defeat in 1954 the Binh Xuyen had sufficient strength, and an interest in protecting a substantial investment, to try to make its own bid for a share of power in the emerging southern Vietnamese state. What role Meyer played with this unsavoury crew has never been absolutely clear. And the question is made more complicated by the certain fact that by this stage of Meyer's life he had already taken a political stance firmly on the left. In this he differed from his employers. The Binh Xuyen were many things but they were definitely not politically conscious leftists.

An aspect of Meyer's personality that was almost instantly apparent upon meeting him was his deeply felt anti-Americanism. What may have been informed gossip attributed this to the closing phases of his career in Vietnam when he was still associated with the Binh Xuyen gangsters. This is a period in modern Vietnamese history that is often ignored. Those with only a passing interest in Vietnam frequently think of a straightforward political process in which the First Indochina War ended and President Ngo Dinh Diem came to power. What in fact happened was much more complicated.

When Diem returned to Vietnam in 1954 he faced considerable opposition; opposition quite separate from his Communist fellow countrymen. It was only with considerable American assistance that he was able to confront and eventually overcome the opposition of two politico–religious sects, the Cao Dai and Hoa Hao which made up a large part of those Vietnamese armed forces that had fought with the French against the Viet Minh and the Binh Xuyen. The final defeat of the Binh Xuyen after heavy fighting in Saigon in April 1955 did not please many of the still large French community in that city. As opponents of Diem these masters of illegality, the Binh Xuyen, were seen as aiding the French in their struggle to retain residual privileges that the Vietnamese leader was determined to end. Whether Meyer was linked to any of the French services which played their secret hands in Saigon at this time has never been clear. The suggestion has been made, however, that American intelligence officials saw Meyer as playing such a role and that, in a crude act of intimidation, they sacked his living quarters in Saigon, damaging or destroying his valuable personal library. If this is true it may, in part, explain the strength of his feeling against the United States, for it was bitter and deeply felt, even obsessional in character.

There is also uncertainty about how Meyer should have been able to move suddenly from his curious position in Saigon to yet again become an 'adviser' to a very different employer in Phnom Penh, this time to Prince Norodom Sihanouk. By the late 1950s, however, this was the role he occupied, and he had clearly become a man of some importance.

Just how important was Charles Meyer? Certainly less important than some, particularly American officials, thought and possibly more important than many of his critics believed. I saw him fairly frequently in 1966 for, of all the Frenchmen resident in Phnom Penh, he appeared to be the only person with an interest in the period of history I was studying and his knowledge of

Cambodia was wide, and in some areas profound. It was during my first meeting with him that I was made aware of just how deeply he felt about America and its policies. I had walked the short distance to his house just around the corner from the Hôtel le Royal in the early evening. Shortly after my arrival it was time to listen to the radio news. The opening item on the news reported a major clash between American and Communist troops in Vietnam in which the Americans had suffered heavy casualties. Meyer's face was transformed, no longer serious and passive but exultant. '*C'arrive*,' he muttered, 'It's happening.' I had a deeper sense than I had ever had previously of what the verb to gloat really means. His gloating was followed by a commentary on the war that would not have done harm to the right-wing image of those old soldiers I had encountered in Paris who still believed that France could have won the First Indochina War. Look at the Americans, Meyer observed, there they are with their massive firepower, their bombing raids, their numbers, and their money. Their money, why it was just as the novelist Jean Lartérguy had put it in his *Paris Match* article, '*Un million dollars le Viet*'. The cost of killing just one Vietnamese was a million dollars, and the Americans were pouring that amount of money and more into their campaigns. And what was it getting them? Losses such as those we had just heard broadcast and no real progress towards achieving their goals. What a contrast it all was with the war the French had fought in Vietnam. The French expeditionary force had not had anything like the financial and logistical backing of the Americans, but it had known how to fight. If only there had been more support from France the result of the war might have been very different.

All this sounded a little strange coming from someone with a reputation for left-wing views, until I remembered that even the French Communist Party had found it difficult to condemn the attempt to reassert French colonial power in Vietnam after the Second World War. When I visited Meyer on other occasions I found that in contemporary terms he was consistently a supporter of leftist positions, and of Chinese positions in particular. He had a Chinese wife and from time to time diplomats from the Chinese embassy in Phnom Penh would be in his house when I called. As the excesses of the Great Proletarian Cultural Revolution became more and more apparent during 1966 I sensed, however, that Meyer's admiration for China was becoming a little more qualified.

As I have already recounted, Charles Meyer was, I believe, the person responsible for my final exclusion from the Phnom Penh archives. Yet I am grateful for assistance that he gave me. Phnom Penh was not an easy environment for research and though I found Meyer's tirades against the Americans unpleasant—for all that I was a critic of the American role in the Vietnam War myself— and his politics unattractive it was useful to be able to hear some of Meyer's comments on Cambodia's history. I was grateful when he found me some genealogical material on the royal family and showed me a copy of King Norodom I's will that had been printed in a French gazette I had not previously seen. Most of all, however, it was fascinating to hear his views of Sihanouk. Adviser he was, exercising some disputed degree of influence over the Prince, but he was certainly no fervent admirer of his patron or of the Cambodian people.

To hear Meyer speak of the 'cretins' he had encountered in the course of some recent journey through the Cambodian countryside was to be transported back in time to the period when arrogant French colonialists made a point of always addressing 'natives' in the familiar form of a verb. When Meyer came to recount the 'stupidity' of a soldier who had barred his way at some point he chose to *tutoyer* the soldier even in his own conversation.

As for Meyer's view of Sihanouk, I can scarcely remember his having a good word to say for him. What he said to me was certainly not what he said to the Western journalists who were suddenly and briefly allowed into Cambodia in May and June 1966. To them he told a different story, with just sufficient indiscretions to make it appear that they were getting close to the 'real' Sihanouk and the 'real' Cambodia. For it was to Meyer that such noted journalists as Harrison Salisbury of the New York Times, I.F. Stone, Bill Stout of CBS, and others were directed. That was the public role. His private views were of a prince who was demonstrating through his current absorption in making films the hereditary lack of mental stability that had plagued the Norodom branch of the Cambodian royal family. There had been a time in Sihanouk's life when he had not been 'serious'. This word has a much deeper connotation in French than in English. What Meyer was referring to were the years before 1950 when Sihanouk came close to deserving his international image as a playboy. Now he was ceasing to be serious again as he wasted his time on the monumental folly of 'Apsara'. After spending large amounts of money on printing presses and to bring journalists from France to staff the *Sangkum* and *Kambuja* Sihanouk had lost interest in journalism. Why, Meyer told me at the end of May, he had himself written the last two editorials in the *Sangkum* that had appeared over the Prince's name since Sihanouk was no longer interested. The Prince, Meyer asserted, was going back to the time when he was 'the little king with his horses and stage shows'.

I suspect that Meyer found it useful to have me as a neutral figure to whom he could vent his spleen. Not that he lacked French acquaintances who would gather for a drink in his house at the end of the day. Nor was it because he hid his irritation with Sihanouk and Cambodia from them. But since they were French, and Frenchmen in Phnom Penh, it was to be expected that they would have their own axes to grind and their own intrigues to pursue. An Australian graduate student who happened to speak French and who had no official connections was a useful object in some ways, even if his growing knowledge of the minutiae of Franco–Cambodian relations in the nineteenth century would in the end have to be brought under control. Moreover, I had come to Cambodia when Meyer was beginning to feel that his own position was at risk; that he no longer was able to exert the influence over Sihanouk that he once had done. He warned that internal dissent could not be long contained and admitted that he feared for his own personal position should there be a significant shift of power in Cambodia's domestic politics.

What had his influence been? Influence is difficult to measure in any circumstances, and in the hot house atmosphere of Phnom Penh politics it was a plant that bloomed and withered with extraordinary rapidity. A reasonable judgment would seem to be that Meyer's influence was never as pervasive as some observers thought, and that even in the years before 1966 it was highly variable in impact according to a whole range of factors. Influencing Sihanouk in any significant fashion meant being able to talk to the Prince and there were clearly long periods when Meyer did not have this sort of access. On other occasions he did have the chance to meet Sihanouk frequently and may have succeeded in moving him closer to the political positions Meyer advocated. In one area that was of great interest to Sihanouk Meyer did undoubtedly exert some influence. As a cartographer Meyer knew about the technical side of mapping and when the Thlok Trach incidents took place in July and August of 1966 Meyer was enveloped in the flurry of activity that followed those border attacks. But it was not only in relation to the technical aspects that he was consulted; he was also busily engaged in writing violently anti-American editorials and *mises au point*. For much of the time, both in 1966 and in earlier years, Meyer's influence was probably fitful and relatively limited, even if, on occasion, it could be significant. If Sihanouk wished to criticise the 'imperialists', then perhaps Meyer's reworking of Sihanouk's ideas into a speech or article may have made the condemnation a little sharper than had originally been intended. His anti-Americanism and his left-wing views at times may have influenced Prince Sihanouk, but never to the degree believed by those who saw Meyer as a man possessing demonic powers.

Given his feelings of deterioration in Cambodia and of his own loss of influence why did Meyer stay? Was he, as some suggested, carrying out other roles than that of being an adviser to Sihanouk? In the nature of things that was the sort of question that could not be asked and has not been answered. My own judgment in 1966 was fairly cynical and I see no compelling reason to revise it now. This man of very considerable ability did not particularly like Cambodians or Prince Sihanouk and had ceased in any event to have very much influence over the Prince. He was locked into one particular sort of double life as a public defender of the regime and as a sharp, even bitter critic in private. I think he was genuine in believing in the virtue of left-wing solutions, and I believe that he admired Communism in China in principle, but the thought of ever having to live there, certainly as the absurdities of the Cultural Revolution became more apparent, scared the wits out of him. For all his complaints I think he stayed in Phnom Penh because, essentially, it was a comfortable place to be and there was no obvious alternative. His job was not too demanding. He was, from time to time, the person about whom foreign journalists gathered, a situation that flattered his ego. And like so many others of his countrymen he had become a man who preferred to live in the East.

A preference for life in the East seemed part of the explanation for Jean Barré's long tenure of the editorship of *Réalités Cambodgiennes*. From this semi-official newspaper it was possible to gauge the shifts and turns of Sihanouk's domestic and international policies; often better than from a reading of the daily Agence Khmère de Presse news bulletin since by the time *Réalités* appeared each Friday Barré had usually had time to sort out the contradictions or confusions that sometimes arose in the course of Sihanouk's extemporaneous speeches and unguarded policy pronouncements. From one point of view the newspaper's title was sharply ironic, for if ever there was a journal that served the purpose of presenting an unrealistic picture of much of Cambodia it was this. In Sihanouk's Cambodia, however, the title had a certain validity. In general when a policy was recorded as being in force the fact that this was noted in *Réalités* was a sign that, for the moment, this was the 'real' decision and alternative points of view had been discarded.

Barré had been in Phnom Penh for years in what must have been a constantly frustrating role as editor of *Réalités*. Fat in 1959, by 1966 he was gross, his flabby body spreading out beneath his bald head and heavy jowls. His background seemed no less mysterious than Meyer's, and Phnom Penh gossip suggested there had been some comparable personal experience in his past that had led him to an equally strong feeling against America. There were those in the French community who hinted at other reasons for his long stay in Cambodia. Admirers of General de Gaulle stated bluntly that Barré had been so closely linked with the Vichy regime during the Second World War that he was safer remaining permanently absent from France. As with so much other Phnom Penh gossip there was no way of being sure where the truth lay. Indeed, even if there were a measure of truth in this allegation Barré would not have been alone among the members of the French community in possessing close links with Vichy. The generation of *colons* who had lived through the Second World War in what had been French Indochina had, for the most part, shown little opposition to the decision that the pro-Vichy Governor General of Indochina, Admiral Decoux, had taken to cooperate with the Japanese to preserve French 'rule' in Vietnam, Laos, and Cambodia. And there were still many of that generation living in Phnom Penh in the sixties.

It was difficult not to wonder whether Barré's sexual preferences provided part of the explanation for his long Cambodian sojourn. He made no attempt to hide his homosexuality and, away from official receptions, he was almost always attended by a young Cambodian companion. The sight could often be a sad one as Barré, flushed with drink, alternately pawed at the young man and regaled him with lengthy commentaries on the international scene. What was sad was not the demonstration of homosexual feeling but the clear indication that so many of Barré's companions gave of their lack of interest in him or his views. Often barely able to speak French they were his companions for a price. To see Barré at the Nouveau Tricotin or La Taverne with his young men barely listening to him or even openly ignoring him to leaf through a crudely printed Cambodian comic book was to be led to think that there indeed had to be compelling reasons for his not leaving Phnom Penh.

Certainly, few envied his job. With a changing succession of assistants it was his task to give an impression of unity and stability prevailing in Cambodia. At times Barré was left to do this without much interference from Sihanouk. At other times the Prince became closely involved, scrutinising copy, altering words, demanding wholesale changes. I sometimes wondered if Barré might not have had the opportunity to exert more influence over Prince Sihanouk than Charles Meyer. Certainly a case could be made that he saw Sihanouk as frequently, and sometimes more frequently than Meyer. If he was in fact able to exert an influence he was certainly more discreet in making any claims to do so than his fellow countryman. Over the years he had been ready to document the achievements of the Sangkum (Sihanouk's mass political movement), to denounce the 'imperialists', most particularly the United States and its Asian allies Thailand and South Vietnam, and above all to praise and defend Sihanouk. Setting the tone for most of the Cambodian press Barré's editorials were a catalogue of Sihanouk's virtues with no hesitancy ever demonstrated in the lavishness of praise or in the use of superlatives.

By 1966, however, Barré too had come to feel that some deep and worrying change was taking place in Cambodia and his caution of other years was now replaced by a readiness to speak critically of the Prince in private. The much praised Prince of the editorials took on a very different guise in conversation. Sihanouk expected him to write the whole of *Réalités* virtually unaided, Barré complained at a reception one evening in June, but then was likely to insist on any number of last minute changes before he was satisfied and the newspaper could go to press. It was harder than ever, Barré went on, to know just what was expected of him. Sihanouk's policies seemed to change from day to day. Was America an enemy or not? No one seemed to know any more. He was expected to provide justifications for contradictory policies that would exhaust the capacities of a Jesuit! Such a case had been the editorial concerning Cambodia's relations with the Vietnamese Communists he had written the previous month. The world was being asked to believe that Cambodian support for the Communists was purely moral in character and had not involved any material assistance; this despite the public gift that Sihanouk had made of food to the National Liberation Front and despite the widespread knowledge in Cambodia that, quite apart from the massive smuggling trade, Sihanouk had authorised at least one major sale of rice to the Communists across the border. As for the Prince's films, *Réalités* was expected to be in the advance guard of those who gushed forth unstinted praise for these . . . . Words for a moment failed him but there was no mistaking the contempt in his gesture. He had had enough, Barré concluded, and he was tired of it all. But like Meyer, he stayed on.

Did it matter that Sihanouk's foreign scribes had become his private critics in 1966? That fact in itself might not have been important, though if Sihanouk had been aware of how they spoke behind his back he might have been alerted to the breadth of discontent and disillusionment that pervaded the country and particularly its capital. For an outsider the contrast between these men's public postures of sycophancy and the private denigration of their employer had a human interest. It was intriguing to note the types of men that Sihanouk employed, to find out who would undertake the tasks assigned them, and to see their reactions to a changing Cambodian political scene. In strictly Cambodian terms Sihanouk's continuing employment of these *plumatifs* in 1966 had a more serious aspect. Charles Meyer might complain that the prince had wearied of journalism in favour of his new passion for film making. But the magazines continued to be published, just as the news bulletin appeared each day, and Jean Barré's *Réalités Cambodgiennes* came out each Friday. None of these publications or the men concerned with their production received the same attention from Norodom Sihanouk as had once been the case. Nevertheless, so long as they appeared they provided the Prince with a framework of illusion that was essential for his personality.

He might only glance at the praise his foreign employees formulated, but clearly he believed it and it sustained him. In 1966, eleven years had passed since he had abdicated the Cambodian throne but this did not mean he had ceased to think like a king. The early years of court life in the 1940s, when he had been treated with the utmost obsequiousness, had left their mark and go far towards explaining Sihanouk's almost absolute incapacity to listen to contrary advice let alone criticism of his policies. In the face of the problems that had grown to such substantial proportions by 1966 Sihanouk had to make public admissions that he would not have conceived of doing before. He admitted the desperate state of the economy; he stated frankly that he had been beaten in his efforts to do something to reduce corruption. Even in the field of foreign policy that he had previously handled with such agility the problems were now much more difficult and he was prepared to admit there were no longer any easy solutions. These admissions made it all the more important for him to have the reassuring praise of his press, which he believed.

There was one final factor that ensured employment for these foreigners who wrote to order. There was little leeway allowed to the men on the left of Cambodian politics who sought to criticise Sihanouk's policies in print. The dangers of attempting to publish a newspaper that offered left-wing solutions to Cambodia's domestic problems had been clearly demonstrated in 1959 when Nop Bophann, the editor of a journal linked to the Communist front Pracheachon organisation, had been killed, it was widely assumed, by Kou Roun's security forces. This warning had later been reinforced when Khieu Samphan, as a young left-wing politician, was roughly manhandled as a warning not to engage in the leftist-oriented journalism of the sort he was associated with as editor of *L'Observateur*. In 1966 Chau Seng's *La Dépêche* was given almost totally free rein to publish what it would on the world outside Cambodia, but the moment there was a hint of criticism of domestic politics Sihanouk unleashed a torrent of threats and warnings. What had emerged by 1966, however, was something new, a newspaper that spoke for the right and was prepared, if ever so cautiously, to criticise the Prince and the policies he pursued. This newspaper was *Phnom Penh Presse* and its chief contributors were a former army colonel, Littaye Soun, and an extremely able lecturer in Phnom Penh University's Law Faculty and member of the Cambodian parliament, Douc Rasy.

More than twelve years later it is difficult to be sure why it should have been that *Phnom Penh Presse* was allowed to publish what it did. The newspaper always stopped just short of outright criticism of Sihanouk by name, but there was never any mistaking what and who the targets of its editorials were. It raised the question of corruption openly and reflected on the dangers to Cambodia of such a state of affairs continuing. By contrast Chau Seng's left-wing *La Dépêche* tried to minimise this issue and to argue that in raising the question of corruption the editors of *Phnom Penh Presse* were, in some very unclear fashion, serving their own self-interest. Even more strikingly *Phnom Penh Presse* offered opinions on the principles of government and the dangers of one-man rule. In Cambodia there could be no doubting the implications of such observations. Sihanouk was reported to be privately furious but publicly he was unprepared to act. The explanation for this unheard of state of affairs probably lay in the Prince's own publicly stated awareness that the most obvious danger to his position in the mid 1960s lay on the right. He did not discount the threat of Communist subversion, but for the moment he accurately saw that the only group with the power to threaten his position was the army with its well-known right-wing bias. Although surprising to outside observers and deeply offensive to Sihanouk himself, *Phnom Penh Presse* had to be tolerated as a sop to the right. But just because it was so deeply offensive Sihanouk felt the greater need for the reassurance provided by the regular eulogies of the press he controlled, the press for which his foreign employees so dutifully wrote. The scribes and sycophants played their parts.

CHAPTER FIFTEEN

A Colonial Connection

Few once-imperial cities proclaimed their former colonial status more plainly than Phnom Penh. Thirteen years after Cambodia had gained independence from France it was still possible to live a very 'French' life in the capital. Breakfast at the Hôtel le Royal could be *croissants* and *café filtre*. Lunch could be eaten at La Taverne. And, for the prosperous, dinner at a price that would have shocked all but the wealthy in a Western city could be had at Monsieur Spacezi's Café de Paris. The night could end at the Bar Jean by the waterfront, a piece of transplanted Marseilles, presided over by the inimitable Jean himself, and his formidable Vietnamese wife. Children of the Phnom Penh elite went to the Lycée Descartes, where all instruction was in French provided by French teachers. The capital's main newspapers were written in French and the importance of the French language was affirmed by the fact that even Prince Sihanouk's Cambodian language newspaper, *Neak Cheat Niyum*, carried substantial French sections interspersed with its material in Khmer. All of this in a city that, no matter how Cambodian its appearance and character away from the old French Quarter, appeared in some areas to have been transplanted direct from Provence to Southeast Asia.

But however striking the architectural links between parts of Phnom Penh and France it was the persistent presence of French men and women in the city that gave such a strong sense of continuing colonialism in the capital in 1966. Just how many Frenchmen there were in Phnom Penh in that year was a matter for debate. The French embassy suggested that the figure for the whole of Cambodia was in excess of three thousand. Non-French observers questioned this estimation and judged that the number was nearer to two thousand than to three. Placed against a total Cambodian population of perhaps six million this did not seem very large, but the importance of these expatriate French citizens went far beyond the simple statistic. They were a highly disparate group. There were the diplomats in the French embassy which was still the largest in Phnom Penh even if the French ambassador no longer automatically took precedence over all other foreign heads of mission as he had done for years after the country had gained independence from France. Moreover, the French embassy of 1966 was a very different diplomatic mission from that which France had maintained into the early sixties. In those earlier years the former colonial connection of the staff members had been emphasised rather than played down. From the ambassador to the lower ranks in the mission service in the former French colonial administration in Indochina had been an essential qualification for appointment. Men who had served as Sihanouk's private secretary or on his personal staff were senior members of the embassy. Others had records of service in different parts of what the French had called 'Our Indochina'. But whether it had been service in Cambodia, or elsewhere in Vietnam and Laos, the colonial past was exemplified in the French diplomatic presence.

French staffing policy for its mission had changed a great deal by 1966, though it was a change that embodied an important continuity. By the middle sixties the personnel of the French embassy in Phnom Penh were very much linked to the French Foreign Ministry, to the Quai d'Orsay, and attuned through a combined personal and political network to the thoughts and intent of the man who occupied the Elysée Palace, General Charles de Gaulle. The old guard of former colonial civil servants had gone from the French diplomatic mission in Phnom Penh, but a French concern to play a leading role in this former colonial possession remained strong. Some would argue that the determination was even stronger once General de Gaulle had consolidated his power in France. He had a personal relationship of considerable importance with Sihanouk, who saw in de Gaulle some kind of a mentor, even a father figure. There was also the deeper aspect to de Gaulle's vision of a French role in the 'Francophone' countries of the world, particularly in Indochina. It was an occasion for world headlines when, in 1965, Charles de Gaulle chose to criticise American policy in Vietnam in terms that abandoned the normal courtesies of diplomatic exchanges between countries that maintained friendly relations. Few, however, who heard or read de Gaulle's words at that time remembered that it was he who had insisted on the policies that led to the outbreak of the First Indochina War, or that it was de Gaulle who, even before the Second World War had ended, had proclaimed, 'If Indochina does not belong to us, to whom can it belong?'

At the other end of the scale from the diplomats were those Frenchmen whose presence in Cambodia defied easy explanation, perhaps verification might be a better term to use. Some were *les anciens de l'Indochine*, the old colonial hands for whom the thought of ever returning permanently to metropolitan France had disappeared years before. A sizeable number of them seemed to be Corsicans for it was from that Mediterranean island that some of the most colourful, if not always the most law-abiding of the *colons* had come in the years before independence. It was no chance matter that in 1966 Phnom Penh's best French restaurant was run by an amiable *Corse*. Similarly, in neighbouring Vietnam, one of his fellow islanders still ran the Continental Palace, the most famous hotel in Saigon. But Corsican or not these men seemed gripped by both a nostalgia for the past and an awareness that in Cambodia they could live a life that would be denied to them in Europe. It was a cycle of daily existence that was untroubled by the demands of climate or of a cold climate at least. Some had found true devotion from their Cambodian or Vietnamese female partners; and for those who had not found this there were easy and inexpensive commercial arrangements that could be made. For some, too, the opium pipes at the end of the day were important, either in the privacy of their own homes or in the famed dim rooms of Mère Chum's that still functioned in 1966 despite the fall-off in foreign clientele in the prevailing climate of economic decline.

If such explanations were relatively easy to offer for the presence of this sort of Frenchman, explaining the economics of their existence was another matter. Were the army or colonial civil service pensions they drew really sufficient to meet the expenses of the old hands? And what of the younger men, those who flew the small aircraft that left Pochentong airport for undisclosed points to the north? It required little imagination and a perfectly acceptable degree of cynicism to give a measure of credence to those explanations suggesting that at least some of these pilots were playing a role in the ever-growing opium trade that had always been part of modern French Indochina and that had assumed a new importance in relation to the Second Indochinese War. Not that Phnom Penh itself was a major distribution point for opium, but the northeast of Cambodia and southern Laos were dotted with obscure and still usable airstrips to which supplies could be brought before being flown or trucked elsewhere.

The French still dominated the rubber plantation industry in the middle sixties and continued to do so until after Sihanouk's overthrow in 1970. One of the largest plantations in the world was located to the east of the provincial centre of Kompong Cham, roughly one hundred miles from the Cambodian capital. This was Chup and in 1966 when I visited it many of the changes of the previous two decades seemed to have passed it by. Once one had driven through the depressingly uniform rows of rubber trees to reach the centre of the plantation one was transported back into the world described so clearly and so acidly by Pierre Boulle in *Sacrilege in Malaya*, his novel about a French plantation in another part of Southeast Asia. Chup was a tropical version of the typical American company town. Status and conformity were everything and if a member of the plantation staff violated the standards of behaviour expected from a person of his status retribution was swift and final. More junior staff members knew how often they could visit the plantation's country club-like sporting complex which was more luxurious than anything to be found elsewhere in the whole of Cambodia. They knew how many drinks they could have in the company-subsidised bar and just what degree of familiarity with the wives of their superiors would be tolerated. And all this was accepted by a Cambodian government that still desperately needed French expertise to run the great plantations, just as it was accepted with apparently open good grace by those Cambodians who had gained sufficient technical expertise to enter the junior ranks of the plantation staff. In 1966 it was accepted without any expectation that they could ever displace or take over from a management that was openly and proudly devoted to preserving French control of the major share of Cambodia's rubber industry.

There were other readily identifiable groups of French men and women forming part of this significant expatriate community. The businessmen had not entirely disappeared in 1966 despite Sihanouk's economic measures, though the fact that there was no longer a Denis Frères office nor a branch of the Banque de l'Indochine was as significant a development in Phnom Penh as would be the sudden removal from modern Hong Kong of Jardine Matheison or the Hong Kong and Shanghai Bank. Frenchmen still played a role in training the Cambodian army, doing so with a remarkable degree of discretion. Apart from the journalists who worked for Sihanouk in various capacities, other Frenchmen worked on contract in assorted Cambodian ministries or were attached to the government as experts in a range of fields. Probably most visible of all in the French community were the teachers who staffed not only the Lycée Descartes, but also many of the positions in the university faculties Sihanouk was so busily and dangerously engaged in developing in the mid-1960s, as well as in other secondary schools in both the capital and the provinces. Some of these teachers had been in Cambodia for years and had gained the affection of generations of students; the same sort of affection that was accorded a woman such as Madeleine Giteau who was the *conservatrice* at the National Museum in Phnom Penh or a man such as Bernard-Philippe Groslier, whose family links with Indochina went back four generations, and who had made such an important contribution to the study of the Angkor complex of which he was *conservateur*. But many of the teachers were in Cambodia only to fulfil their national service obligations and, along with many others of their countrymen whose association with Cambodia could be either short or long-term, they were remarkably prone to offer criticism. In 1966, just as in earlier years, it was not necessary to spend a great length of time in the company of French men and women to hear the frequently repeated judgment: Cambodians have a slave mentality!

The implications of this judgment went beyond the private complaints of those who worked in Sihanouk's employ to publicly praise him and his country only to criticise in private. It was a reflection of a much deeper facet of the French relationship with the whole of Indochina, not just with Cambodia. Planned as colonies of settlement, areas to which Frenchmen in substantial numbers could go as they had to regions of North Africa, particularly to Algeria, none of the countries that made up French Indochina ever became such a colony. Yet the rhetoric of French discussion of the Indochinese region in colonial times never quite abandoned the view that the territory of Vietnam, of Laos, of Cambodia had in some way become French, and in more than a merely legal sense. This was the sort of thinking that lay behind de Gaulle's statement made towards the end of the Second World War and the policy he instituted after it. It was also the thinking that lay behind a wider, less directly political attitude that was adopted by French men and women of all ranks in the expatriate community right up to the granting of independence that took place in 1953 and 1954. In a way that I believe goes far beyond the attitudes adopted by the British in India or Malaya, to take only two 'Anglo-Saxon' examples, the French thought of themselves as not only ruling but also as possessing Indochina. It was *theirs* and this allowed them to adopt a clear-eyed view that they were present as colonisers essentially for *their* own benefit. This attitude also led them to formulate views of the Cambodians that were dismissive in a contemptuous fashion seldom equalled elsewhere in colonial experience, even by their fellow 'Latins'. In the late nineteenth and early twentieth centuries French officials had seen nothing extraordinary in the pursuit of policies that they judged would lead to the extinction of a Cambodian national identity as the result of Vietnamese immigration into Cambodia. It was the same cast of mind that allowed French observers—devotees of Cartesian thought, supposed connoisseurs of Angkorian civilisation —to dismiss Cambodians as a force to be seriously reckoned with in terms of a history that had led them to think like slaves. The tragedy was that too many Cambodians were ready either to believe them or to act as if they did.

Probably only the passage of time has made clear the extent to which Cambodia in 1966 was still not a truly 'decolonised' country. To write in these terms is not to accept uncritically the arguments of the left, whether the Cambodian left or the left composed of outside observers with that political persuasion. But it does involve underlining the degree of both conscious and unconscious readiness on the part of a whole range of Cambodians in 1966 to remain in what can only be described as a quasi-colonial relationship with France. This observation is true whether one is talking of Sihanouk and of his unreal belief that France could in some unclear fashion extricate Cambodia from the international perils that daily seemed to grow more ominous, or talking of that section of the Cambodian elite who were probably more at home using French than their own language. It is also true when one is talking of a government that was not concerned about the fact that Phnom Penh's Catholic cathedral was part of a French diocese, or of an important number of leftists who were ready to seek their political future in association with the French leftists of Paris than the Cambodian Communists who had made clear their commitment to revolution by going into the *maquis*. Most of all, in terms of Cambodia's short-term future, Sihanouk's decision in 1966 to look towards France as his country's new 'First-Friend'—for years China had been given the honour of that title —underlined a prevailing mode of thought that was marked by a failure to break with the past rather than by the pursuit of policies that offered a real assurance or hope for Cambodia's future.

In 1966 no single political event, either domestic or international, so preoccupied the Cambodian administration as the visit of President Charles de Gaulle. To understand why this should have been so it is necessary to summarise the essentials of Sihanouk's foreign policy as it developed in the late 1950s and early 1960s. Stated baldly Cambodia's foreign policy was based on Sihanouk's belief that his country could only survive as an independent entity, dominated neither by Vietnam nor by Thailand, if it were protected by a major external power. At first Sihanouk had thought that it would be possible to have China play the role of Cambodia's protector while at the same time still justify his country's claim to neutrality through maintaining diplomatic relations with the United States and other Western powers. The difficulty with this calculation was that it only provided an answer to Cambodia's external problems so long as the international situation in the Indochinese region remained static. By the early sixties such a hope could no longer be held. Increasingly, in Sihanouk's judgment, the involvement of the United States in the Vietnam conflict was leading to the prospect of an eventual Communist victory, a threat of the most serious proportions. At heart Sihanouk had the gravest misgivings about such an outcome but he was quite unready to join his country to the American camp in an effort to contain Vietnamese Communism. In 1964 sharper and sharper disagreements over American policy in Vietnam led to Cambodia's breaking diplomatic relations with the United States, and so to the removal of one of the factors that could balance potential Communist power.

In these circumstances Sihanouk more than ever looked to the Chinese as an assurance against Vietnamese domination. Despite the increasingly close links between Phnom Penh and Hanoi, and Phnom Penh and representatives of the southern National Liberation Front, Sihanouk and his closest advisers distrusted the Vietnamese and saw their country's salvation lying in the protection afforded by close friendship with China. By 1966 this policy posed grave problems. As the war in Vietnam grew ever more intense, a development carrying with it both the long-term threat of Communist victory and the short-term dangers of fighting spilling over into Cambodia's territory, the first stirrings of the Great Proletarian Cultural Revolution called into question China's capacity to play any significant role in determining events in the Indochinese countries. Small wonder, perhaps, that Sihanouk gave such a hearty welcome to the indication President de Gaulle gave of his readiness once again to become involved in the complex problems of Indochina. For Sihanouk, and doubtless for de Gaulle himself, the possibility of the French president appearing as a *deus ex machina* had to be welcome.

But what, in fact, did de Gaulle have to offer? Only when this question is posed does it become clear that Sihanouk's hopes and de Gaulle's convictions concerning his and his country's power of determining events in Indochina were essentially hollow. General de Gaulle's immense personal prestige was not accompanied by any real leverage in relation to either the Vietnamese Communists or the Americans. Sihanouk's hopes that the contrary might be true, that the former colonial power could, thirteen years after independence, reassume the role of protector bore little if any relation to the harsh realities of international politics. Instead of making judgments founded on reality Sihanouk's hopes reflected a mixture of desperation and a continuing readiness so common to his generation to turn to France for guidance when grave problems had to be faced.

President de Gaulle's visit to Cambodia was set for late August 1966. For months before this date, however, preparations for the great occasion were in train. The Cambodian secondary education system came to a virtual halt, so far as instruction was concerned, as thousands of school children were mobilised to perform in mass pageants and gymnastic displays. Nothing captures the flavour of this mass activity and of a Cambodian unconfident readiness to rely on France better than Sihanouk's decision to have de Gaulle greeted upon arrival at the 'Olympic' stadium by a member of the Royal Socialist Youth declaiming an ode to the French President. Having decided this should take place the job of composing a suitable poem of praise was passed to a French schoolteacher rather than to one of the many perfectly competent Cambodians who could have undertaken the task. There was sadness as well as irony in the vision of a member of that curiously named group standing before tens of thousands of his compatriots to greet de Gaulle in the name of Cambodia in words written by a Frenchman.

Before General de Gaulle could be hailed as the 'great son of France', however, a mass of other preparations had to take place. There was an enforced exodus from Phnom Penh of those Frenchmen whose past and present political beliefs were seen as inimical to those held by the French president. Some were required to go no further distant than the seaside resort of Kep. Others, it appears, were told to absent themselves from Cambodia altogether for the duration of the visit. Familar faces suddenly disappeared as the day of de Gaulle's arrival drew nearer. The most prominent *émigré* of all was Dr Grauwin, the famed 'Doctor of Dien Bien Phu' whose experiences at that French defeat in Vietnam had made him a critic of French governments of every hue and a quintessential representative of those in Cambodia's French community who never thought of returning 'home'. But as the *émigrés* departed so did temporary replacements surge in as the French press in all its manifestations flocked to cover the event. Newspapermen bedecked with expensive cameras, television technicians making arrangements to shift their cumbersome equipment from point to point, *grands reporters* ready to provide instant analysis 'in depth' all came to Phnom Penh. There was a carnival atmosphere at the Hôtel le Royal as the austerity of the previous months was for a little while forgotten and as the hostesses from the bars still functioning in the capital found themselves fêted in a fashion that most of them had feared would never occur again following the break with the United States in 1964.

Yet however much Sihanouk hoped General de Gaulle's visit would make a significant contribution to Cambodia's security there is still uncertainty as to the extent that the French president planned his visit with this aim uppermost in his mind. At least as important was de Gaulle's hope to play a part in relation to the growing crisis generated by the war in Vietnam. If he had been successful in attempting such an initiative Cambodia might, indeed, have benefited. But nothing of real importance emerged as the result of de Gaulle's foreign minister, Couve de Muirville's, meeting with a Hanoi representative during the course of the visit to Phnom Penh. As for direct relations with Cambodia, what de Gaulle had to offer was certainly more meagre than Sihanouk had hoped whatever he said publicly. France, de Gaulle told the Prince, would aid Cambodia to build a phosphate factory. It would finance the establishment of a second French *lycée*. And France would make a gift of uniforms to the Cambodian army. Of these three forms of aid the latter was without doubt the most significant. The inability of the Cambodian army to meet even the costs of clothing its soldiers was a significant cause for resentment among all ranks in the armed forces. The promised phosphate factory mattered little, in the short-term at least. As for the promised further *lycée*, such a project may have suited de Gaulle's vision of the expansion of 'French civilisation' at the same time as it accorded well with Sihanouk's passion for an increase in the quantity of young people passing through secondary institutions. In terms of Cambodia's real needs, and given the already clear resentment that was felt by students who were unable to find jobs to go with the qualifications they gained as they were force fed through the country's secondary schools, de Gaulle's offer should have been seen as dubiously necessary, at best, and as dangerous, in terms of creating an even larger number of unemployed but educated youths, at worst.

When General de Gaulle left after having made the obligatory visit to Angkor, a temporary feeling of euphoria prevailed among those who made up Sihanouk's inner circle. Had not the leader of one of the great countries of the world come to Cambodia and shown his support for Sihanouk and his policies? Euphoria faded quickly, however, as the lack of substance to the visit became apparent. De Gaulle could speak with an independent voice, criticise the United States, approve of Sihanouk's policies, and have his ministers make contact with representatives of the Vietnamese Communists. He could do all this in a former French colonial possession, using the language that remained important for the Cambodian elite, but he could not guarantee Cambodia's security. Just as important, the fillip de Gaulle could give to Sihanouk's depressed personality while the visit was in progress had little if any carry over into domestic affairs when once again these affairs became a demanding aspect of Cambodian political life as preparations were made for the September 1966 elections.

Because this commentary on Franco–Cambodian relations has included some sharply critical observations concerning the persistence of quasi-colonial attitudes in Cambodia there is a point in stressing once again that not all French men and women behaved as if the achievement of Cambodian independence in 1953 had no significance. Nor did all Cambodians share Sihanouk's hope and belief that his country could find security in association with a France led by General de Gaulle. Among the older, conservative Cambodian elite matters were undoubtedly complicated by the memory, held even by those who were critical of France and the French community in Cambodia, of the role France had played a century before. In the early 1860s French intervention, however self-interested, saved Cambodia from what seemed to be the prospect of certain eclipse as the kingdom faced threats to its existence from Thailand in the west and Vietnam to the east. But however much such considerations weighed in the minds of older Cambodians there is no doubt that the members of the slowly emerging left saw matters differently. Just as Father Tep Im, as the result of a very different commitment, deplored the continuing role of the French Catholic Church in Cambodia so did the men and women of the left see in the continuing importance Sihanouk attached to the French a further testimony to the impossibility of achieving their radical goals other than by radical means. As with so many other aspects of Sihanouk's Cambodia, the French connection could not be other than deeply offensive to the Cambodian left-wing.

When Sihanouk was overthrown by right-wing plotters in 1970 a France no longer led by Charles de Gaulle could play no part in preventing Sihanouk's downfall. As the supremacy within the movement fighting against the Lon Nol regime in Phnom Penh passed into the hands of the most radical revolutionaries France could do little to influence the course of Cambodian affairs. Yet as the final tenuous links with the country's colonial past were snapped and destroyed France did have one last role to play in Cambodia's affairs. When Phnom Penh fell to the Cambodian Communist forces on 17 April 1975 it was to the French embassy compound that foreigners of all nationalities, not just Frenchmen, retreated while protracted negotiations were undertaken for their exodus. France therefore played a final part in the drama that brought an end to one form of Cambodian existence and ushered in a new Kampuchean society. But the role France played in the grim days of April 1975 was far removed from that which Sihanouk had so fervently desired less than a decade before. As with so many other aspects of Cambodian life and politics in 1966 the French connection was misjudged by Sihanouk and seen in very different terms by his dedicated left-wing opponents.

CHAPTER SIXTEEN

The Hereditary Enemy

Some little time after his deposition in 1970 Sihanouk, then living in Peking as a Chinese pensioner, described himself to a Western journalist. He was, he told his visitor, *un bon khmer*, 'a good Cambodian' literally, but a phrase that is probably better rendered as 'a real Cambodian'. In no way was this more true than in his attitude towards the Vietnamese, a people that he had on many occasions during his long political career stigmatised as the hereditary enemy. In 1966, four years before his sudden downfall, Sihanouk had shown himself to be a real Cambodian, certainly a real Cambodian ruler in terms of historical precedent, in another way. While never ceasing to think of the Vietnamese as enemies he sought through diplomacy to find ways to keep these enemies from absorbing Cambodia. The way to do this, he believed, was to make his ethnic enemies political friends. It was a fateful choice, one that played a major part in his own overthrow. It was also a decision that underlined a dilemma in terms of ensuring Cambodia's national existence: how was Cambodia to contend with a geographical neighbour whose population was so much greater in size and whose leaders for centuries had pursued policies leading to the progressive absorption of Cambodian territory?

Vietnam was Cambodia's hereditary enemy, yet in 1966 it was extraordinarily difficult to move beyond an awareness of this basic fact to a more detailed understanding of the nature of relations between Cambodians and Vietnamese. Part of the reason for this difficulty lay in the fact that there was a substantial minority of Vietnamese residents in Cambodia who, though they were subject

163

to various forms of discrimination, appeared to live in relative peace, if not amity, with their Cambodian neighbours. At first glance the presence of this highly visible minority seemed to quality Sihanouk's insistence on the Vietnamese as enemies. If one could understand the politics behind Sihanouk's publicly stated policy of support for the Vietnamese Communists, was this nonetheless not a contradiction of his own insistence on the basic enmity of his country's eastern neighbour? There was much that was unclear.

The historical record was straightforward enough. Viewed in historical perspective Cambodia had been the long-term loser in an unequal contest over the centuries as the Vietnamese in the east and the Thais in the west had eaten away at the territories of the once powerful Cambodian empire that had flourished in Angkorian times. The fact that Cambodia had faced threats from both the Thais and the Vietnamese was a theme that was repeated almost endlessly in Sihanouk's speeches. Moreover, by the middle 1960's these enemies to the east and west were both allied to the greatest 'imperialist' power of all, the United States; at least *some* of the Vietnamese were allied to the United States, and their even more feared Communist compatriots appeared to be growing in strength.

While it suited Sihanouk's political purposes to bracket the Thais and Vietnamese as enemies, this was a simplification of history that he probably did not believe himself. Certainly many of his politically conscious countrymen rejected the idea of there being little if any difference between the potential danger posed by the Thais and that posed by the Vietnamese. Thailand and Cambodia had on frequent occasions in the past been in conflict, but there was no basic cultural division between the two countries. This was a fact my researches had emphasised time and again. As recently as the late nineteenth century tens of thousands of Cambodian peasants had moved from Cambodia into Thailand to escape from the death and destruction that accompanied the one great challenge mounted by Cambodian forces against French rule in the 1880s. A few years later at the end of the nineteenth century, to the surprise and dismay of French officials in Cambodia it was revealed that many of King Norodom I's close advisers were men who had been born in Thailand and who, despite decades of service to the king in Phnom Penh still thought of themselves as Thais. By contrast, in those areas of northwestern Cambodia that had come under Thai suzerainty in the late eighteenth century, Cambodians drawn from the great semi-hereditary ruling families continued to administer the land for the Thai kings in Bangkok. Indeed, when a Thai royal commissioner visited Battambang in the late nineteenth century and, in the words of a French observer, 'debauched' the ethnic Cambodian governor's daughter and subsequently refused to marry her the governor had no hesitation in chasing his royal Thai master's representative from his territory. The governor owed allegiance to Bangkok but as a Cambodian he was master of the province. In short, and whatever the difficulties of the past and present, Cambodians did not think of the Thais as fundamentally and irretrievably racial enemies. Prince Sisowath Entaravong spoke for many others when he told me one day that in Bangkok he felt completely at home.

The Thais on occasion might have been Cambodia's bitter enemies, and at the best of times there was a Thai tendency to regard Cambodians as country cousins, less civilised and lacking in self-discipline. But this did not stop Cambodian kings from regarding the Thai court as a model for what the Cambodian court ought to be. Nor did it make Bangkok any less important a centre of Buddhist scholarship for Cambodian monks. It was impossible to imagine a Cambodian speaking in similar terms about the Vietnamese or Saigon. Thailand was not a place apart. Vietnam was.

A basic and essentially unbridgeable gap existed between Cambodians and Vietnamese. The population of each country represented two fundamentally conflicting cultures; the Cambodians an Indianised culture and the Vietnamese a Sinicised culture. The differences between these two cultures had very practical implications. When the Vietnamese absorbed Cambodian territory they sought to transform it into something that was 'standard' Vietnamese. They sought to do this behind clearly demarcated frontiers. The Cambodians, even when they had been powerful, had not thought in these terms, neither had the Thais. For the Thais and the Cambodians, both beneficiaries of Indian ideas on statecraft, frontiers were regarded as porous and shifting and new populations that might come under the control of the state as the result of conquest were not of necessity to be moulded into some pale imitation of the conqueror.

Nothing was more clearly marked in the Cambodian mind than the practical implications of their differences from the Vietnamese that had been revealed during the terrible period in the 1830s and 1840s when Vietnam occupied much of modern Cambodia and sought to transform the state. By the 1820s Cambodia was at one of the lowest points of its long history. The royal family was split into contending factions with some princes looking to Bangkok for support while others sought aid from the Vietnamese court in Hué. In the 1830s the Vietnamese emperor, Minh Mang, struck against Cambodia, invading the country and placing a puppet queen on the throne. For nearly a decade the Vietnamese worked to eliminate Cambodia's distinctive identity. They required the wearing of Vietnamese dress by Cambodian officials and the adoption of Vietnamese methods of administration. They struck at the Cambodian Buddhist church, the repository of so much that was essential to Cambodia's sense of national existence. In doing this and more, they finally sparked a Cambodian rebellion that was supported by the Thai court in Bangkok and led to the reestablishment of a quasi-independent Cambodia, dependent on both Bangkok and Hué it was true, but with its survival at least temporarily guaranteed by the interest both Vietnam and Thailand had in seeing Cambodia play the role of a buffer state.

To suggest that many Cambodians remembered the details of this terrible period would be misleading. But there was quite certainly a memory of the essentials. Vietnam had sought to destroy Cambodia. The Thais had helped Cambodia to survive. And then the French had come as colonialists to institute a ninety year period which put an end to the threats that both of Cambodia's neighbours had posed in the past. This was how many Cambodians thought of the past, and it is certainly how French history books present the picture. But there was more to the story, even if once again the details were not always clear in Cambodian minds. The French had ensured Cambodia's survival it is true. In doing so, however, they quite deliberately followed policies that further aggravated the difficult relations existing between Cambodians and Vietnamese.

Buried in the archives in both Paris and Phnom Penh are

documents that tell the story in remarkable detail. Once established in both southern Vietnam and Cambodia the French as colonial masters looked askance at what they saw as the tawdry Cambodian court and the feckless Cambodian population. They had little love for the Vietnamese, but they believed them to be an 'intelligent and industrious race', in sharp contrast to the 'decadence' of the Cambodians who had 'fallen from their antique splendour'. Nothing seemed more proper in the eyes of the French officials of the nineteenth century, with their un-selfconscious belief in a crude form of social Darwinism, than that the Vietnamese should be encouraged to settle in Cambodia and by swamping the Cambodian population transform the country. Only with major Vietnamese settlement, the French judged, could Cambodia become economically productive.

With such thoughts as stated policy the French looked with pleasure on the influx of Vietnamese, who from the 1880s onwards, came in increasing numbers to swell the existing community of their compatriots who had long been settled as fishermen and small artisans along the riverine areas about the Mekong and its tributary the Tonle Sap. From the beginning of the twentieth century, as the French colonialists became more and more involved in the day to day administration of Cambodia, it was Vietnamese who filled the subordinate ranks of the French colonial civil service. Vietnamese acted as the clerks, the messengers, the postmen and the telegraphists, filling roles that Cambodians were either unable or unwilling to fill. Even before the turn of the century a Vietnamese had assumed the despised duties of the French administration's executioner, erecting and dismantling the guillotine used to despatch rebels and murderers in a location a little outside Phnom Penh.

This immigration and later natural increase brought the Vietnamese community in Cambodia to a total of some four to five hundred thousand by the 1950s. It also provided the base from which the Communist Vietminh drew recruits during the First Indochina War. This fact was a further cause for Cambodian distrust of and enmity towards the Vietnamese. For although Sihanouk from the early 1950s onwards worked vigorously for an end to French control over his country neither he nor the great majority of his countrymen looked favourably on the efforts of the

Communist Vietnamese. As later events have proved, the relatively few Cambodians who were ready at that stage to embrace Communism, were at one with their more conservative compatriots. One of the bitter complaints of the Pol Pot regime, before it was overthrown, was that even during the fight against the French the Vietnamese Communists placed their interests, and those of their country, above the interests of the Cambodian Communists within Cambodia.

With the First Indochina War ended and with Cambodian independence achieved the problems posed by the existence of a major Vietnamese community resident in Cambodia remained. Legislation preventing their holding certain kinds of employment did something to thin their numbers, but by 1966 there were probably still three hundred thousand Vietnamese resident in Cambodia. They continued to be fishermen and artisans, and it was still Vietnamese who provided the bulk of the labour for the great French-controlled rubber plantations that had been established in Cambodia immediately after the First World War. Most important, they remained a community apart. This was true in almost every aspect of life. The Vietnamese who were members of the Catholic church had, Father Tep Im assured me, virtually no contact with the small Cambodian Catholic community. Even if they were members of families that had been settled in Cambodia for several generations they seldom spoke more than a smattering of the Cambodian language, and their priests were Vietnamese who had as little to do with their Cambodian brother priests as the laity did with Cambodians. At the highest levels of Cambodian society one could find occasional examples of marriage between a Cambodian and a Vietnamese as education and wealth provided a means to bridge the gap that otherwise divided the two ethnic groups. But intermarriage was rare, much more so than was the case for the Cambodian minority community resident in Vietnam. Unlike the Chinese in Cambodia, many of whom had been assimilated, the Vietnamese remained separate and apart, a readily identifiable and, in Cambodian eyes, despised alien group. If it was an expression not often heard in official usage, Cambodians in general still thought of the Vietnamese in a pejorative and traditional description: the Vietnamese were the *yuon*, the hated 'barbarians'.

Most of this was clear to me before I returned to Cambodia in 1966. Once back in Phnom Penh it did not take me long to find that a section of the Vietnamese community resident in Cambodia was ready to proclaim its political sympathies for the Communist fight against the Saigon regime and its American supporters. This pro-Communist group expressed its political sympathies in the newspaper *Trung Lap* (The Neutralist), the only Vietnamese language newspaper published in Phnom Penh, and a journal that was singularly misnamed. It took its news and its political position straight from Hanoi and catalogued the successes and the heroism of the Communist forces fighting against the Americans and their 'puppet allies'.

This kind of commentary on the events taking place in Cambodia's eastern neighbour fitted well with much of the official propaganda put out by Sihanouk's own Ministry of Information, but it was hard to believe that members of the Cambodian elite were reassured by such clear evidence of the presence in their country of supporters of Vietnamese Communist policies. Just how many of the Vietnamese in Cambodia did fall into this category? No one ever seemed very clear, though perhaps the best estimate I received came from a member of the Vietnamese minority whose own background and political stance set him far apart from his leftist compatriots.

Bertin Minh's name made clear the sort of Vietnamese he was —one of that small but important group of southern Vietnamese whose families had gained French nationality in the first two or three decades of the twentieth century. Such men and women were to be found much more readily in Saigon than in Phnom Penh, and it was through an introduction provided from Saigon that I had come to meet Bertin Minh. He spoke of himself as a man without politics, but almost immediately went on to point out that not to take sides was a luxury open to few Vietnamese living in Cambodia. He doubted if the supporters of the Communist cause were more than a third of the Vietnamese resident in Cambodia, but they were an active and outspoken group, and probably growing in number. The Cambodian security forces might succeed in preventing them from affirming their beliefs in any very public fashion, but this did not prevent them from urging their views on their fellow Vietnamese. Though Bertin Minh did not say it,

Sihanouk had made no secret of his view that Vietnamese Communists acted as essential if unloved go-betweens linking Cambodian Communists with the powerful leadership of the Vietnamese Communists in Hanoi.

The younger members of the Vietnamese community, Bertin Minh went on, were increasingly attracted by the Communists and their propaganda. The deep antipathy between Vietnamese and Cambodians was a fact of life for the members of his community and the young resented the curbs that independent Cambodian governments had placed on their occupying certain kinds of employment. They admired the exploits of their countrymen fighting in Vietnam itself. The combination of being members of a disadvantaged community in Cambodia and of their Communist compatriots' success in defying the might of the United States and its Saigon allies made Communism appear almost irresistible. He himself could resist, and would, but he doubted the costs were worthwhile and, like his relatives in Saigon, he had begun to think that an uncertain future in France, taking advantage of his French nationality, was a lesser risk to take than living through an even more uncertain future in Cambodia.

As for the rest of the Vietnamese community living in Cambodia —the two-thirds not committed to Communism if his estimate was correct—Bertin Minh found it difficult to predict their future. They did not have the option of retreating to France as he did. They lived in Cambodia because it was a country at peace, and one in which some had enjoyed modest economic success in the past. But they lived, all of them, with an unspoken concern, even fear, for their future. They all knew that as Vietnamese they were a target for Cambodian distrust, and even worse.

Bertin Minh provided one Vietnamese view of his compatriots living in Cambodia. The longer I spent in Cambodia in 1966 the clearer it became to me that the Cambodians whom I met with any regularity seldom spoke of the Vietnamese, whether those in Cambodia or those in Vietnam, in any detailed fashion. It was not the case, of course, that they had no feelings about the Vietnamese but rather, if my judgment was correct, that their feelings were widely and uniformly held; views that did not need expression. The Vietnamese were despised, distrusted, and feared. Members of the Cambodian elite might have Vietnamese friends, particularly the older members of that group since many of them had been educated at schools in Saigon while the French still held power. Or they might have come to know Vietnamese as fellow Indochinese while studying in France. But such relationships were exceptions. The Vietnamese who had been fellow students at the Collège Chasseloup–Laubat in Saigon were, in the eyes of the Cambodians, scarcely 'real' Vietnamese. The real Vietnamese were the dangerous and threatening Communists, the less threatening but equally untrustworthy representatives of the Saigon regime, or the resident Vietnamese minority in Cambodia that was always to be distrusted as a possible advance guard of their much more numerous compatriots across the border. The Vietnamese, it became clear, were thought of as a race, not as individuals. Indeed, the individual Vietnamese that my Cambodian acquaintances knew and accepted could occupy that role just because they were seen as departing from the firmly held stereotyped view.

Everything seemed to suggest that the stereotype of the Vietnamese held by the Cambodian elite was shared, in its essentials, by the peasantry. No doubt there were and are qualifications to be entered here also, but the evidence of Cambodian recent history seems to confirm the presence of the peasants' racism that was always waiting to break out in times of crisis. The horrifying massacre of Vietnamese civilians in Phnom Penh and elsewhere by Cambodian troops shortly after Sihanouk was turned out of office in 1970 was all too clearly a reflection of the deep feelings against these culturally separate members of a distrusted immigrant group.

It was against this background that Sihanouk in 1966 embarked on a desperate program to forestall what he feared would be an eventual threat from a united Communist Vietnam. By early 1966 he was convinced that sooner or later the American backed Saigon forces would be defeated. In these circumstances, he argued, it was essential to come to terms with the Vietnamese Communists and to persuade them in advance to recognise Cambodia's territorial integrity. Given the course of subsequent events this appears as one of the Prince's more astute judgments. But the problem was how to achieve his goals. He made no secret of the fact that he was supping with the devil and only had a short handle to his spoon. Even more to the point in terms of his own future, the decision to try to come to terms with the Vietnamese Communists, however much it represented a modern variant of strategies followed by his royal ancestors in the past, contrasted with the deeply held feelings and judgments of his conservative advisers. Sihanouk was convinced he could come to some form of mutually advantageous agreement with the Vietnamese Communists. For the most part, the conservative elite on which he was so dependent did not share that point of view.

Since 1964 Sihanouk had been slowly but surely moving towards a closer relationship with the Vietnamese Communists, but now in 1966 he took a series of decisions that made his intentions much clearer. In April the commercial mission that the Democratic Republic of Vietnam (the government in Hanoi) had maintained in Phnom Penh for some time was given permission to elevate its status to that of a 'representation', something short of a full embassy status, but a clear diplomatic gain for the Communists nonetheless. At the same time Sihanouk announced his hopes of signing agreements with representatives of both Hanoi and the South Vietnamese National Liberation Front that would ensure the integrity of Cambodia's borders. To give material support to these instances of his goodwill Prince Sihanouk announced that his government was making a substantial gift of food to representatives of the National Liberation Front. Less publicly he authorised the clandestine sale of rice to the Communist forces operating in southern Vietnam, so giving an important degree of tacit official support to the already rampant trade in smuggled rice.

Despite these gestures, and despite the frequent suggestions that mutually satisfactory border agreements were about to be concluded, Sihanouk did not achieve his aims in 1966. It was not for want of urging on his part. His chief negotiator, Sarin Chhak, was later to tell me in Paris that he and his fellow Cambodian representatives had found themselves under growing pressure from the Prince to conclude an agreement with the Communists, even if in their judgment too many concessions were made to the Vietnamese. They resisted, and the Vietnamese were, in any case, such difficult adversaries with whom to deal that it was not until the following year that both the government in Hanoi and the representatives of the National Liberation Front finally pronounced their support for Cambodia's existing boundaries.

Sihanouk was to hail this as a triumph, but quite apart from the question of just what the Communist avowal meant and in particular whether it covered the always contentious issue of offshore islands, by the time agreement was announced in June 1967 there were many of Sihanouk's one-time supporters who had come to question the cost that was apparently being met in order to achieve supposed Vietnamese assurances of future good behaviour. What is more, even before the end of 1966 Sihanouk had himself come to wonder about the wisdom of the strategy he was following. The fact that he clearly had begun to have doubts only served to reinforce the misgivings of his associates. What, they asked, was the point of negotiating for some future readiness on the part of the Vietnamese Communists to honour Cambodia's borders when, with the Prince's agreement, Vietnamese Communist troops were already making widespread use of the less settled areas of Cambodia's eastern territories as rest and staging areas and as part of the great supply route running down from northern Vietnam, through Laos, to the south?

There are many ways of looking at the policy Sihanouk attempted to follow towards the Vietnamese Communists from 1966 onwards. Some saw him then, as they continue to do more than twelve years later, as a victim of circumstances faced with impossible choices. Others might make harsher judgments, arguing that he quite deliberately chose to follow a path that carried with it the greatest possible risks, not just for himself but for his country as well. In terms of his own position in Cambodia the judgments of those who had once been his most important supporters became increasingly critical between 1967 and 1970. Beyond all the personal rivalries and self-interested motivations that were without doubt of great importance, the failure of Sihanouk to show that his policies towards the Vietnamese Communists would succeed was a major factor that tipped the balance of conservative opinion against him in March 1970. Lon Nol, Sirik Matak and their supporters were without doubt naïve, just as they were later to prove to be incompetent as leaders of the country. But they were briefly at one with the population in whose name they acted when, in 1970, they expressed their disapproval of the large-scale presence of Vietnamese Communist troops in Cambodia, blamed Sihanouk for the situation, and sought, ineffectually, to have the troops leave.

Their actions engulfed Cambodia in the Second Indochina War in a way that it had managed to avoid previously. The Vietnamese Communists responded by throwing their support behind the scattered Cambodian Communist units and this, in turn, brought the American and Saigon regimes' invasion of Cambodia a little more than a month after Sihanouk's downfall. Sihanouk had sought to find a way to reconcile the hereditary enemy in 1966, but in a manner that plainly recalled the problems his country had faced in relation to Vietnam in the past he had little leverage with which to achieve his aims. The plotters who succeeded him tried to expel the Vietnamese Communists, only to find that their hopes were no less ill-founded than Sihanouk's. With the tragic irony that has so often been part of Cambodia's recent history the regime that defeated Lon Nol and finally came to power in Phnom Penh in April 1975, just five years after Norodom Sihanouk's deposition, proved itself to be essentially Cambodian in one way if no other: The Pol Pot government was just as convinced as its predecessors that the Vietnamese were the herditary enemy. Unlike its predecessors, however, it was this new and brutally radical government that was to experience the ultimate proof of the validity of their countrymen's traditional fears. Barely two months before the Vietnamese invaded Kampuchea to support a hastily constructed rebel front, the Pol Pot regime published a 'Black Book' that commenced with a denunciation of Vietnamese aggression in terms devoid of ideological content but laden with the basic, long-held Cambodian view of its neighbour. The nature of Vietnam and of the Vietnamese, the 'Black Book' states at the very beginning, is that of 'an aggressor, an annexationist, and a devourer of the territory of other countries'. Sihanouk's fears of 1966 had been realised.

CHAPTER SEVENTEEN

The Elections

So much was happening in Cambodia in 1966 and so many events and developments were of great importance that there is a risk of being trapped in the snare of an excess of superlatives. It is hard, however, not to see the Cambodian parliamentary elections of September 1966 as one of the most important events in a very important year. Indeed, given the path of Cambodia's politics after 1966, a strong case could be made for regarding the September elections as *the* most important event of the year. The story of the elections and the background to them can, nevertheless, be told fairly briefly.

Elections had always played a significant part in the public politics of Sihanouk's Cambodia. This was not because Sihanouk was in any real sense a believer in democratic ideals, in fact quite to the contrary. It seems almost certain that the slow development of Cambodia's political life in the years immediately after the Second World War left Sihanouk convinced that anything like Western parliamentary democracy was to be avoided at all costs. For during the years between 1946 and 1952, a period when Sihanouk grew slowly to political maturity, the factious nature of Cambodian politics in an elected parliament had been demonstrated time and again. Groups that called themselves 'parties' formed and split, constructed political alliances and immediately reneged on the agreements that had formed the basis for cooperation. Having come to recognise his own potential for political action and aided at this stage by a few shrewd older advisers, King Sihanouk, as he still was in 1952, assumed all power and set about

175

gaining independence from France while embarking on a period of personal rule over the kingdom.

On the external front Sihanouk was successful when France granted independence to Cambodia in November 1953. Internally, matters were not so clear. Sihanouk was without doubt the dominant personality in Cambodian politics. But he still had to face the existence of a hostile political opposition. He found a brilliant but, as it proved, essentially short-term answer to his country's internal problems in 1955. The answer was in two parts. First, he abdicated the throne in his father's favour. The benefits of this decision were many. Most important Sihanouk was able to play a much more active role in politics than had been possible while he was still king. Yet, at the same time, he continued to benefit from almost all of the prestige that went with being king. Secondly, he formed a political movement, the Sangkum Reastr Niyum (People's Socialist Community). This was, he insisted, a mass national movement and not a party. Sihanouk was right to insist on the Sangkum's being a mass movement and not a party. Loyalty to Sihanouk and his policies was essential for membership and a range of politicians from the far right to the overt left found it possible in 1955 to take the necessary oaths affirming, whether genuinely or otherwise, such loyalty. In September 1955 Sihanouk's Sangkum candidates won a stunning victory in the elections held that month, gaining all of the seats in the National Assembly and over eighty per cent of the votes.

But what did this all mean? From Sihanouk's point of view it should have meant that he had a tame parliament cleansed of factional in-fighting that seemed the chief characteristic of previous Cambodian political life. Old rivalries, however, persisted. This was reflected in the fact that no less than nine ministeries took office and then fell between September 1955 and January 1958. Something had to be done and Sihanouk, still at this stage an activist, decided what it was. He announced that the number of deputies in Cambodia's National Assembly would be increased in order to reflect the expanded size of the electorate resulting from the right to vote being given to women. This decision had to be confirmed by a referendum and the result was decisively positive in favour of Sihanouk's proposals. With this success behind him Sihanouk decided that in the new elections to be held in March

1958 he personally would choose the Sangkum candidates. Opposed only by a weak Communist front organisation called the Pracheachon, Sihanouk's candidates swept into parliament with an official margin of no less than ninety-nine per cent of the votes.

The success of his hand-picked candidates in the 1958 elections and his own personal success in a further referendum held in late 1959 confirmed Sihanouk's belief in the utility of referring matters to a national vote. But he did not see such voting as having the power to change his policies. He wanted deputies in the National Assembly who would endorse his policies, not men and women who would question them. He was ready to put the question of who should lead Cambodia to a national referendum, but at the time there could never have been any doubt about the outcome, quite apart from the widespread instances of officials acting in a variety of illegal ways to ensure the Prince achieved the best possible result. In short, the Prince saw elections as part of a national ritual, not as a process that could greatly affect his determination of policy. He would hand-pick candidates and they would be elected to serve him. The fact that elections took place had importance, but it was of a very different importance from that given to elections in the West.

The elections held in September 1966 were to elect a new parliament replacing that elected in June 1962. When the 1962 elections had been held Sihanouk had once again given his personal approval to the candidates of the Sangkum, and he had shown his continuing readiness to play the left off against the right by endorsing a number of well-known younger radicals as well as the generally conservative bulk of the candidates. The most important of these younger radical candidates were Khieu Samphan, Hu Nim, and Hou Youn, men who were later to play such an important part in the campaign to overthrow the Lon Nol regime after Sihanouk's fall in 1970.

Whatever hopes he may have held for the country and for his own position at the beginning of the sixties, the years between 1962 and 1966 had not been good ones and in the face of the troubles he and the state confronted, the Prince in August 1966, the month before the elections, made a momentous decision. For the first time since 1955, he announced, he would not be personally selecting those who would be the Sangkum's candidates for election. This was a stunning development and I found that its importance was immediately and widely recognised by all who took an interest in Cambodian politics. There could be no doubt what the decision meant in terms of the outcome of the election. The way was now open for the most conservative forces in Cambodian politics to buy their way into parliament. And this was, for the most part, what happened. It was not only votes that were bought, a wealthy conservative determined to gain a parliamentary seat also bought off his opponents. Oh yes, my princely friend told me on the day the elections were held when I met him at a small party, there was no doubt about this being a widespread practice. He could not, for the life of him, see why any of his compatriots wanted to become deputies in the present difficult and even dangerous phase of Cambodian politics, but apparently it was important enough for them to pay out substantial sums of money to achieve their goal. A payment of one hundred thousand riels—nearly fifteen thousand American dollars at the realistic black market rate of exchange— was a common enough way of ensuring that a possible rival did not stand in the way of a candidate's success.

Other unorthodox means had been used too, it seemed. Although the Prince's decision to avoid personal involvement in the elections had been a calculated decision favouring those on the right of Cambodian politics, there was one man of conservative views who was capable of angering Sihanouk as much as his critics on the left. This was Douc Rasy, one of the editors of *Phnom Penh Presse,* the right-wing newspaper that had throughout 1966 made increas- ingly clear its opposition to Sihanouk's policies and his style of government. In some mysterious fashion candidates opposing Douc Rasy suddenly appeared in his constituency armed with tape- recordings of speeches Sihanouk had made attacking the con- servative editor several months before. These tapes, one of Sihanouk's advisers told me, had to have come from the Ministry of Information, and it did not seem unreasonable to suppose that the decision to make them available to Douc Rasy's opponents came from the Prince himself. As a tactic it failed, for whatever Sihanouk's opinion of him Douc Rasy's constituents saw him as a man genuinely concerned to promote their interests.

Even stronger measures had been employed to try to prevent Khieu Samphan from being returned to parliament. Phnom Penh gossip was of constant petty harassment that became more serious interference when some of Khieu Samphan's campaign workers were detained by the security police in an effort to strike a major blow at the young left-wing politician's chances. But as was the case with Douc Rasy, Khieu Samphan was returned to parliament with a comfortable majority. His reputation for incorruptibility and the evidence he gave of genuine concern for the poor provided him with more than enough support to overcome the heavy-handed interference of Kou Roun's men.

Although the September elections brought into being a new parliament with a strongly conservative character it would be wrong to think that the election itself was contested in any very clear ideological terms. The Governor of Kratie province, Ok Nall, was probably right when he said in a private commentary on the results that these were best interpreted in terms of personalities than policies. Economic issues may have played some part in particular constituencies. Ok Nall confessed he was puzzled about one result in Kratie town itself. A man whom Ok Nall termed a 'leftist' had campaigned vigorously and been returned to parliament on a platform that consisted of sharp criticism of the rises that had taken place in the cost of living. Seeking the votes of men and women who were in one way or another linked to rice production he promised the scarcely realisable combination of increased rice prices and a fall in the cost of living.

The absence of a campaign cast in ideological terms did not remove the ideological importance of the election result, or the immediate and longer-term importance for Sihanouk's position in Cambodia. The men of wealth who were ready to buy their way into parliament in 1966 may not, in general, have been able to give an account of their political beliefs couched in ideological terms. Their conservatism was more fundamental, not a cerebral thing delineated in textbook fashion. They were instinctively against change, concerned with retaining power, little moved by calls for aid to the weak and needy, and deeply disturbed by the path Sihanouk had been following in both domestic and external politics since the early sixties. At the time they were elected they probably had little sense of how they might translate election into action, since they knew of the limitations Sihanouk had been able to place on parliament's political power. Whether or not many of them realised it, what the elected conservatives of 1966 needed was a leader, a man who would be prepared to risk Sihanouk's disfavour by pursuing policies even if the Prince disagreed with them.

Within less than a year a leader, or group of leaders, had emerged that showed a readiness, at first hesitantly but increasingly with assurance, to follow policies in which they believed, whether or not these pleased the Prince. The final policy decision taken by these men, final in terms of Sihanouk's Cambodia, was the decision to depose him in March 1970. It was a decision that was overwhelmingly supported by the conservative Cambodian parliament which had been elected in September 1966. Such a final result of his readiness to let the conservatives come to power had clearly never occurred to Sihanouk in 1966. Later he was to admit that he was 'unpardonably naïve' in trusting General Lon Nol and in believing that under Lon Nol's leadership the Cambodian army would never turn against him. This was Sihanouk's judgment on himself after he fell from power. Like many of Sihanouk's political commentaries, however, it only tells part of the story. He was naïve, certainly, but his naïveté was compounded by the fact that his decision to opt out of deciding who should be the Sangkum candidates in 1966 was a highly self-interested decision. He acted as he did in 1966 because he saw this as the road to self-preservation, both in personal and political terms. Sensing that his policies had steered Cambodia into a dead end he looked to the right to give him time to find new ways to deal with new problems. But most particularly he saw the right as ready to maintain him in power. What might have happened if he had made a different choice can never be known. What is clear is that in acting as he did and so permitting the conservatives to triumph in the 1966 elections he opened the way to his own political demise. He did even more, for the incompetent Lon Nol regime that toppled Sihanouk from power proved unable to do more than preside over the dissolution of the Cambodian state as a prelude to the emergence of Communist Kampuchea.

CHAPTER EIGHTEEN

Point of Departure
Point of No Return

No amount of reassessing the past or of gaining new insights as the result of the passage of time, will lead to the year 1966 being seen as *the* period that ensured a Communist victory in Cambodia and the planned and unplanned tragedies that followed that event. Whether we will ever be able to understand the dynamics of the Cambodian or Kampuchean revolution once it gained momentum following Sihanouk's overthrow is an open question. To write history historians must have sources and the difficulty of obtaining adequate and trustworthy source material for the period between 1970 and 1975 cannot be exaggerated. As for the years immediately after the triumph of the Communist Party of Kampuchea in 1975, it may simply be the case that there will always be massive gaps in our knowledge of much that happened, and why.

The importance of 1966 does not lie in its providing any total explanation for the succeeding decade of Cambodia's political history. Within a shorter time frame, however, for the period that led up to Sihanouk's fall from power in 1970, what happened in 1966 can be seen to have been of fundamental importance. Even for the longer term, developments that took place during this year cast shadows, not always sharply defined, that suggested the possible shape of Cambodia's future. Above all else 1966 can be seen as the year when Sihanouk's control of the Cambodian state ceased to be certain. It was the year when, for the first time since the country attained independence in 1953, it became possible to think seriously of Cambodia without Sihanouk. This, as much as anything else, explains why so many people in 1966 were ready

181

to talk frankly about the political and economic issues that dominated their lives. Without knowing when or how it would come, there was an underlying recognition that change, and possibly momentous change, was on the way.

Robert Shaplen, an able American observer of Southeast Asian affairs once wrote that 'Cambodia is Sihanouk'. This comment was both true, and misleading. In terms of foreign policy from the attainment of independence until the middle sixties a broadly accurate picture shows that no foreign policy decision of consequence was made other than by Sihanouk. Domestic politics were another matter. Because Sihanouk was the dominant factor in Cambodia's internal politics for so long there was a readiness on the part of even the best informed observers to concentrate on the Prince's role to the near exclusion of other individuals and less obvious factors. Sihanouk can never be removed from any account of Cambodia's post-independence politics, but future reassessments may have him less constantly occupying a centre stage position, especially in domestic politics.

What I believe the events of 1966 demonstrated was the extent to which Sihanouk's options had been exhausted. The basic policies, both domestic and external, that he had formulated in the middle and late 1950s, no longer answered the changed circumstances of the middle 1960s. Sihanouk found himself forced to choose between making new approaches to Cambodia's growing range of problems, or adopting a policy of doing nothing and hoping that difficulties might disappear as events took their course. As it happened, Sihanouk followed both these courses of action with increasingly dangerous results for his own position.

Because Sihanouk remains the focus of attention, no matter what qualifications are entered to downgrade his importance, some attempt to assess his and Cambodia's position in the years leading up to 1966 is essential. For it is only against the background of the previous decade that the true importance of 1966 is revealed. Central to these earlier years is the fact that, for a period, Norodom Sihanouk *was* a highly successful leader. Without indulging in the excessive praise that was so much a part of Cambodian official life, there can be no doubt that Sihanouk played an indispensable role in persuading France to grant Cambodia independence at the time it did. Once that independence was achieved the then King Sihanouk decided to abdicate the throne and to bring to an end the factious nature of Cambodia's internal politics by forming a mass political movement which incorporated politicians of widely differing opinions. This was a brilliant decision. At the same time as Sihanouk pursued these internal policies he appeared, until the early sixties, to have found a formula that would guarantee Cambodia's exclusion from the increasing conflict that affected his Indochinese neighbours. Never truly neutral, Cambodia nevertheless appeared for a period to be successful in balancing East against West basking in China's favour but receiving major aid from the United States.

The problem was that the success of both Sihanouk's domestic and external policies depended on the situation remaining static. The extent to which Sihanouk realised this is simply not clear. But once again the importance of 1966 can be seen in the fact that by the end of that year Sihanouk seemed to realise that all of the old options had been used up and new approaches had to be made. This must not be taken to mean that 'blame' or 'fault' can be assigned in such a way that Sihanouk, alone, was responsible for the deteriorating situation in which Cambodia found itself by 1966. Because he insisted on being *the* dominant figure of Cambodian politics there is no way that Sihanouk can avoid a major measure of responsibility for much that happened so long as he held power. But attention must also be given to the changes which took place that were fundamentally outside his capacity to control. Most particularly many events in the international field were, from the early sixties onwards, increasingly moving in directions that Sihanouk could neither affect nor control.

Prince Sihanouk often spoke publicly of his lack of formal education, of how he never read books, of his reliance upon instinctive action rather than decisions based on a careful review of alternative possibilities. In making these comments on himself he spoke no less than the truth, but he was a man who had absorbed an essential piece of historical knowledge: he knew that Cambodia's modern history had been one of almost continuous decline and that, barely one hundred years before independence was regained in 1953, the country's very existence had been in question. Aware of this, Sihanouk's foreign policy was directed towards one aim: the preservation of Cambodia's territorial integrity. The problem was how to pursue this goal.

Initially the strategy that Sihanouk devised accorded well with the existing international circumstances. Proclaiming Cambodia to be neutral, despite strong pressure from the United States to join the anti-Communist camp, Sihanouk sought to have his country's security assured by accepting aid from both the East and the West. In the atmosphere of the late 1950s this led to competition between the United States, the Soviet Union, and China to outdo each other in the provision of economic and military assistance of various kinds. Basic to Sihanouk's calculations was the belief that should a major crisis ever develop Cambodia would have the support of China. This belief was made the more important because, in the final analysis, Sihanouk saw the ultimate threat to Cambodia as coming from Vietnam united under Communist rule. Whatever denunciations Sihanouk made of Thailand and its intentions towards Cambodia and however much the United States became an increasing target for Sihanouk's anger from the early sixties, Vietnam was seen as the real and most dangerous enemy.

Sihanouk's policy of seeking to balance one ideological group against another, of accepting aid from all who were prepared to give it, and of proclaiming Cambodia's neutrality worked well so long as the situation in Vietnam did not pose any real threat to Cambodia. Until the early sixties this was the situation that existed. Sihanouk and his government might be highly critical in public of the growing role of the United States in Vietnam, but privately they were not displeased if an American presence was effective in blocking the reunification of the whole of Vietnam under Communist leadership. In fearing such an eventual outcome to the developing war in Vietnam Sihanouk was undoubtedly relying on his instinctive judgment. It seems highly unlikely that he arrived at his conclusions as the result of detailed arguments in position papers, or sustained analysis. Rather, his instincts told him (correctly in the long-term) the United States would eventually be defeated in Vietnam and the result of that defeat would be the outcome most threatening to Cambodia. From 1963 onwards, therefore, he began a slow shift towards a policy of open friendship with the Vietnamese Communists and increasingly his relations with the United States were marked by bitterness and mutual lack of understanding. The final outcome was the rejection of United States aid in 1963, and subsequently the breaking of diplomatic relations with the Americans in the following year.

The removal of an American presence from Cambodia altered the balance of forces within the country and the previously existing basis for Cambodia's international position. Ever more convinced that the Americans would be defeated in Vietnam Sihanouk began a slow programme aimed at ensuring that the results of this projected defeat would not be Cambodia's domination by a Communist Vietnam. Efforts were made to improve and build on existing relations with the Vietnamese Communists. The Cambodian government's acquiescence in the active border smuggling was directly related to Sihanouk's belief that the Vietnamese Communists had to be kept favourably disposed to his country. Discussions were begun with the Vietnamese Communists to try to resolve long-standing border disagreements between Cambodia and Vietnam. But at the back of all this Sihanouk continued to distrust the Vietnamese and hoped that, if a crisis should take place, China would be Cambodia's protector.

The major problem for Sihanouk was that by 1966 his external initiatives did not appear to have any guarantee of success and, most important, developments in Cambodia's international relations were having increasingly significant effects on the country's domestic affairs. In the long run Sihanouk's estimation of the likely course events would follow in Vietnam proved correct. Even if it was the result of instinctive judgment he was proved right in believing the United States would end its involvement in a war that was dubiously winnable and which finally came to divide American society. But by 1966 his earlier estimations no longer seemed so assured of being correct. This was the period of American escalation and Sihanouk began to wonder whether the United States might not after all succeed in propping up an anti-Communist southern Vietnamese state. He sought to keep his options open by a proclaimed sympathy for the Vietnamese Communist cause and by continuing negotiations with them in an effort to settle border issues. But he could no longer be sure of what would happen in Vietnam. His growing uncertainties in this regard were made the more disturbing as China entered the disorganised period of the Great Proletarian Cultural Revolution. To place alongside the nightmare image of a Communist Vietnam Sihanouk now had to consider the almost as disturbing possibility of a surviving southern anti-Communist Vietnamese state, backed by the United States and hostile towards Cambodia for the support it had given to its Communist enemies. The policies that had seemed to work so well for nine or ten years after independence no longer seemed to answer the country's needs.

Cambodia by 1966 was a very different country from that which Sihanouk had dominated until the early 1960s. Most important, Cambodia by 1966 was a country marked by substantial discontent, particularly among those who were in a position to pose a threat to Sihanouk's position. Picking a single cause or even the major cause for Sihanouk's eventual deposition in 1970 is a dangerous exercise. But there is little doubt that in any explanation of that event the part played by the Cambodian army as the result of its discontent with Sihanouk's policies has to be given great importance. It does not seem that Sihanouk had ever calculated the impact on the army of his decision to cut off American aid to Cambodia, neither had he subsequently understood what the ending of American aid had meant to the army. Sihanouk did not see army camps such as Kim Kosal's that I visited in June 1966. He did not know, or did not want to know, of the problems caused by the lack or run-down of equipment, of the lack of uniforms, of the unavailability of funds to pay for maintenance, or of the difficulties cause by barely sufficient fuel supplies. Here was a combination of Sihanouk's unreadiness to face harsh facts and his advisers' reluctance to tell him the truth. What made the situation more dangerous was that Sihanouk had no doubts where the political sympathies of the army lay. He knew the sympathy of the officer corps was with right-wing politics. But he neither knew the full details of the army's deteriorating position nor believed that Lon Nol, as head of the army, would ever turn against him.

A case can be made that in the face of Cambodia's multiple difficulties Sihanouk simply gave up and that his near obsession with film making was the visible sign of his unreadiness to try to contend with the country's problems. To a degree there is some truth in this analysis. Whether consciously or otherwise, Sihanouk's involvement in film making did represent a retreat from reality. The situation was, however, more complex than such an analysis suggests. By 1966 Sihanouk was increasingly unwilling to involve himself in the details of administration and he was reluctant to take broad policy decisions. Nevertheless, he was not ready to give up power. Sihanouk knew that the nationalisation and austerity measures had not been successful, and he was aware that corruption abounded; his policies were being criticised by both the left and the right but he was determined to remain Cambodia's leader. Confronting this dilemma, he made his choice in 1966; he chose to link his own political future with the right. Even if they were men on the right such as Douc Rasy who were ready to criticise his policies, Sihanouk believed that Cambodia's conservatives were his natural allies, and this was the thinking that led him to allow the elections of September 1966 to go forward without his usual procedure of designating who should be the candidate to represent the Prince's political movement, the Sangkum.

In choosing the conservative forces in Cambodia's politics to bolster his position Prince Norodom Sihanouk signalled his unwillingness to seek a compromise with the left. For the best known leftists still active in Cambodia's overt political life the developments of 1966 promised an increasingly menacing future. Before the succeeding year had ended many had fled into the countryside to prepare for a revolution that probably came sooner than most of them expected.

For Sihanouk, for his fellow countrymen, and for Cambodia as a state 1966 was a year when the politically conscious took stock and made fateful decisions. The drift towards chaos and disaster had gone too far to be ignored and with politics a real and open issue in Cambodia Sihanouk made clear that in the future his sympathies would lie with the right. He saw the right as being ready to preserve his position, even though he continued to make minor gestures to leftist policies. Despite the erosion of his position and knowing that it was only the men of the right who could at this stage bring him down he still made his choice. Just as his slow shift towards a reversal of the foreign policy positions he had adopted over the preceding five or six years represented an indication that he had exhausted his options, so did his decision to move to the right in domestic terms rob him of the opportunity of manoeuvre that had once been his. That he recognised this to some extent was revealed in the anguished speeches he made in the closing months of 1966 when he spoke of the potential ruin facing Cambodia. He was now forced to admit that he could no longer automatically order the state as he wished.

The fact that time, and Sihanouk's options, had run out was what I had been observing during the months I spent in Cambodia in 1966. Present in the country as a student of nineteenth-century history the events taking place were more momentous than I realised at the time and the significance of much of what I heard or saw or had mentioned to me escaped my full understanding. For a man such as Prince Sisowath Entaravong who spoke so gloomily of the future and was, in his own unspectacular and infinitely courteous way so representative of conservative interests, a period had come when if the right did not act only disaster could follow. For men on the left, whether Cambodians or otherwise, 1966 had a different meaning. For a left-wing foreigner such as Charles Meyer the prospects seemed clearly set for a rightist success that would topple Sihanouk and his stable of advisers. Yet for Poc Deuskomar, and for others whose names I did not then know, the dangers of 1966 offered possibilities for the future. The right might be threatening and Sihanouk could be moving towards policies that would appease conservative forces. Convinced as they were of the correctness of their left-wing analysis, however, from 1966 onwards men like Poc Deuskomar increasingly took to the *maquis* not only to preserve their lives but also because of their conviction that radical left-wing change would eventually come to Cambodia.

None of these domestic developments could, of course, be separated from the international pressures that also grew so much greater after 1966. The Second Indochinese War grew in intensity and became a vital, even integral factor in Cambodian politics, strengthening the right and finally leading Sihanouk to acquiesce to Richard Nixon's secret strategic bombing of eastern Cambodia. Whatever other factors were involved, and there were many, the plot that was finally mounted by men of the right to bring down Sihanouk in March 1970 resulted in part from the alarm the conservatives, and particularly the army officer corps, felt as tens of thousands—the Pol Pot regime claimed in its 'Black Book' that there were more than a million—of Vietnamese Communists occupied large areas of Cambodian territory. Cambodia was deeply involved in the Vietnam War and Sihanouk's opponents on the right believed he was to blame for this situation.

Could it have all ended differently? The student of history has no satisfactory answer to this question, for an attempt to review what might have happened must always founder on the rocks of actual events or be lost among the conflicting currents of alternative possibilities, none demonstrably and finally more certain to have occurred than another. What may be argued with some confidence, however, is the fact that the developments of 1966 *were* a vital step towards the ultimate disaster that finally overtook Cambodia. This observation is not a mere historical truism. The developments of 1966 were critical to the course Cambodian history took up to Sihanouk's overthrow in a way that events of previous years had not been. The right in Cambodian politics was in the saddle, ever more firmly following the elections of September 1966. As the dominant political force, the right followed programmes and policies that only accelerated the coming clash with the still small but growing number of men and women who had come to see Cambodia's salvation in terms of Communism.

How is one to explain what happened after Sihanouk's downfall? This will be a task that will occupy historians and political analysts for years to come. Because of the lack of sources or because of their unreliability, there seem likely to be gaps and uncertainties that will never be filled or removed. What I witnessed in 1966 was a prelude to the emergence of Communist Kampuchea, a prelude of the greatest importance. Although I had no way of sensing the path that Cambodia's politics would follow once Sihanouk no longer led the state I did perceive that great change was on the way and my final journal entry reflected this:

Returning to Cambodia after a long absence it is impossible not to be struck by the changed atmosphere of the country. There is discontent, and there is a surprising amount of open speculation about the possibilities of change in the direction of the country . . .

If Sihanouk remains in the saddle, perhaps with his feet no longer in the stirrup irons, his tenure is threatened by factors that he seems unable to control. The irony of the situation is that the factors most likely to bring change result from the implementation of policies that are essentially Sihanouk's own . . .

If one wants one word to summarise, I would pick 'fluid'. Basically, all situations are fluid, but it is the infinitely greater degree of fluidity which I find most striking . . . there is no doubt in my mind that Cambodia has reached stage one in a move towards change.

In 1966 Sihanouk in one of his rare moods of confidence said that he could rule Cambodia because he knew the 'veins of our nation' well. Almost a year later he issued a desperately phrased challenge. 'Let those who disapprove come and take my place or do away with me!' Less than three years passed before the men he thought faithful to him took up his challenge. They were able to remove Sihanouk, but they could not replace his state with one they were capable of controlling. Their opponents, the final victors in April 1975, were to give proof that they could and would impose a new style of government and were ready, as they put it themselves, to sweep away two thousand years of history. Nineteen-sixty-six was only one of those two thousand years but in terms of Cambodia's modern history it truly was a year that represented a point of departure and a point of no return.

AFTERWORD

Kampuchea 1979

The Cambodia of 1966 has vanished forever, and tragedy has followed tragedy. The cost of the war that raged in Cambodia between 1970 and 1975 can scarcely be exaggerated. It was not merely brutal, since all wars are brutal. This conflict provided an opportunity for that darker side of the Cambodian character to assert itself in the lack of any restraint and in the deliberate use of political violence and of terror by both sides. For the Lon Nol forces the routine execution of prisoners and the savagery directed at non-combatants was probably seen as nothing more than the way in which any war should be fought, particularly a civil war where the enemy was in league with the hated Vietnamese. For the Cambodian Communists the deliberate use of political violence and of calculated terror may at first have been an essential weapon of the weak. Later it was used more readily as the result of the frustration at being unable to gain victory despite the military ineptitude and what the Communists believed was the utter moral and political bankruptcy of their opponents. It was also surely a reaction to the terrible bombing of Communist-held regions that went on until August 1973.

How the Khmer Rouge survived that aerial bombardment we may never know, for during that period more bombs were dropped on Cambodia than on Europe throughout the entire period of the Second World War. But survive the Khmer Rouge did, only to find that for twenty long months of bitter frustration the Lon Nol forces were able to stave off ultimate disaster. When defeat for the Lon Nol forces came it was at the hands of an army numbering at most sixty thousand, an army of peasant boys and youths ready to carry out unquestioningly the post-war orders of leaders committed to transforming Cambodia.

Just as there is much that we do not know about the conduct of the war in Cambodia between 1970 and 1975, so it seems likely that the outside world will never know in satisfactory detail what happened next. Some things seem clear enough—Phnom Penh was forcibly evacuated; existing patterns of a Cambodian society with roots stretching back more than a thousand years were ended at a stroke; the Buddhist church ceased to exist; money as a means of exchange was eliminated. And we know that the population laboured long hours in the fields working towards agricultural self-sufficiency and a new programme of irrigation. But we will never know just how many Cambodians were killed. The evidence is overwhelming that very many were killed as a matter of policy. Whether this policy reflected central government direction or whether it was the decision of local authorities may never be clear, and policy may well have varied from place to place and from time to time. The numbers killed cannot have been less than tens of thousands and could well have involved hundreds of thousands. This is before an account is taken of the costs in human life exacted as the result of rampant disease.

The government led by Pol Pot, the *Angka Loeu* or 'High Organisation' to use the term by which the Cambodians knew it, proclaimed its intention of breaking totally with the past and seemed to have no hesitation in pursuing policies to ensure the success of this decision. In one way, however, Pol Pot and his colleagues acted in strict accord with Cambodian traditions. They regarded the Vietnamese as their country's sworn enemy, and from mid-1977 they increasingly backed their judgment with force. Here, again, we may never know just what caused the Pol Pot regime to follow the policy it did. It was one thing to see the Vietnamese as a dangerous enemy and another to commit the numerically weak forces of their army, however motivated they may have been, against the most powerful war machine in Southeast Asia. It is simply not enough to note that there were outstanding border disputes that needed resolution. Nor is it sufficient explanation to see Kampuchea's Communist leaders deciding that it was better to strike first against an enemy that had traditionally followed policies that ended with the annexation of Cambodian territory. To know that the historical record is one of long-term enmity is quite different from mounting assaults against vastly superior numbers and refusing to enter into negotiations. For an outsider the policies of the Pol Pot regime appear irrational. To see the policies that the Communist leaders of Kampuchea pursued as rational would be to accept their standards and their logic.

At last there came the Vietnamese response, a decision to find a final solution to the problem posed by Kampuchea. This decision was full of echoes since Minh Mang, the Vietnamese emperor, had similarly ordered the occupation of Cambodia in the 1830s. How much of the traditional nineteenth-century attitude concerning Cambodia prevails among the Vietnamese leadership? If they were frank, would their position differ from the views expressed by the great mandarin Phan Thanh Gian in the early 1860s? Ingenuousness did not disguise the basic meaning of his words concerning Cambodia and the Cambodians:

> In principle our intention is not to take possession of this country: we wish, following heaven's example, to allow the population to live and exist in peace. We do not wish the loss of this little kingdom as do some others [he meant the Thais] whose hearts are full of malice.
>
> The Cambodians are savages whose nature is bad and vicious; as often as they submit so often do they rebel, but they constantly forget the rule and the law.

The Vietnamese have occupied a shattered country and placed their Cambodian government in Phnom Penh to attempt the awesome task of rebuilding a society. In early 1979 it is impossible to judge whether a Cambodian or Kampuchean society can be rebuilt for we do not know what remains from other days. It is almost impossible to know the results of the Pol Pot regime's forty-four months of rule over Kampuchea, or to discover what happened as hundreds of thousands were forcibly moved into the countryside to work in the vast collective units that rejected old ways of life and old forms of family organisation. It is also impossible to know how many lives were taken through executions and disease.

Cambodia has experienced a sustained dreadfulness that can never be adequately chronicled. It has been a dreadfulness that has a character seemingly far removed from the twentieth century, for all this century's range of horrors. It is not hard to think of Kampuchea between 1975 and 1979 as a country that knew the kind of horror a writer attempted to convey when, fourteen hundred years ago, he sought to capture some sense of the aftermath of the first Saxon revolt in Britain. Writing in about 540 AD and describing the fate of the population the monk Gildas recorded: 'There was no burial save in the ruins of the houses, or in the bellies of the beasts and the birds.' For Kampuchea we might add: 'And we do not know if there is hope for the future.'

Cambodia 1984

Cambodia's political future is as uncertain in 1984 as it was in 1979. Vietnam continues in occupation, propping up a client government, and opposed by Cambodian resistance forces. A political solution to Cambodia's problems is not in sight.

In contrast to the political uncertainties associated with Cambodia's future, one thing does seem clear. The Cambodian people have slowly, and with great difficulty, clawed their way back from the brink of the demographic disaster that they faced in 1979. Along the Thai-Cambodia border in late 1979 one could witness scenes of horror that evoked memories of other great human tragedies, when famine and brutality had reduced men, women and children to skeletal figures, some literally dying on their feet. Not all of the refugees who crossed into Thailand in 1979, or who sheltered in squalid camps along the border, were victims of extreme hunger and disease. Many were, however, and to visit a camp such as Sokh Sann, as I did in December 1979, was to see desperately ill and wasted beings who looked like inmates of some ghastly Asian Belsen.

Slowly, and as the result of major international aid efforts, the picture has changed. What has not changed, and never can, is the toll of death that was the legacy of the Pol Pot years. In 1979, I wrote that we will never know how many died while Pol Pot ruled over Cambodia. That statement remains true today. A range of figures have been offered as estimates of the death toll caused both by executions and by the disease and hunger that stalked the harshly regimented lives of the Cambodians forced into unremitting agricultural labour by the Democratic Kampuchean regime. Some observers have suggested as many as three million died who, in other circumstances, would have lived. Others have calculated that *only* five hundred thousand died.

The evidence will never be clear-cut, but my own estimation is that the cost in lives of the 1975-78 period in Cambodia was around one million, with as many as half of those victims being executed. The reasons for suggesting this figure are many and complex, but one of the reasons for arguing that a million died lies in the evidence I collected in 1980, while working as a consultant for the United Nations High Commissioner for Refugees. Interviewing in camps up and down the Thai-Cambodian border, I found the suggestion made by some observers that Pol Pot's victims had been drawn almost exclusively from the Cambodian bourgeoisie was simply not true. In a sample of one hundred refugees, selected so as to minimise reliance on information from the former bourgeoisie, I found that no fewer than forty persons had lost close family members through execution, to a total of eighty-eight victims. Of these forty who had suffered such losses, over half were peasants or low-level urban workers.

Eighteen months later, in September 1981, I travelled through Cambodia and saw and smelt the mass graves that were being exhumed to reveal the hundreds upon thousands of skeletons, most with shattered skulls, for execution by bludgeoning the victims to death was the preferred way for killings to be carried out — the cost of execution was minimised in this way, since to have used bullets would have been too expensive. I saw the slaughter house in the Phnom Penh suburb of Tuol Sleng, where torture for days, or even weeks, was the fate of thousands, particularly officials, whose loyalty to the regime had come into question.

Human resilience and the will to live has triumphed over this tragic past. The Cambodian population is growing once again. But their country has been changed forever.

INDEX

ABOUT THE AUTHOR

Milton Osborne is an internationally recognized authority on the history and politics of Southeast Asia, and in particular Cambodia, a country with which he has had an association for forty-four years since being posted to the Australian Embassy in Phnom Penh in 1959. A graduate of Sydney and Cornell Universities, Dr Osborne carried out research for his PhD in Cambodia in 1966, during which time he kept a journal that forms the basis for much of the present book.

Dr Osborne has held academic posts in Australia, the United States, the United Kingdom and Singapore. A consultant to the United Nations High Commissioner for Refugees in relation to the Cambodian refugee problem in 1980 and 1981, he was Head of the Asia Branch of the Australian Government's Office of National Assessments from 1982 to 1993. Since 1993 he has been a full-time writer and consultant on Asian issues. In addition to the present volume, he is the author of the following books and monographs on Southeast Asian subjects :

The French Presence in Cochinchina and Cambodia: Rule and Response, (1859 1905), 1969.
Region of Revolt: Focus on Southeast Asia, 1970. Revised and expanded edition, 1971.
Politics and Power in Cambodia: The Sihanouk Years, 1973.
River Road to China: The Mekong River Expedition 1866 1873, 1975.
Southeast Asia: An Introductory History, 1979.
Sihanouk: Prince of Light, Prince of Darkness, 1994.
The Mekong: Turbulent Past, Uncertain Future, 2000.
Exploring Southeast Asia: A Traveller's Guide to the Region, 2002.

Research Monographs :

Singapore and Malaysia, 1964.
Strategic Hamlets in South Viet Nam: A Survey and a Comparison, 1965.